With love –

Jacinta Yang.

TAKE CHARGE

Reclaim Your Life and Be Your True Self

Jacinta Yang

10-10-10
Publishing

Take Charge: Reclaim Your Life and Be Your True Self
www.JacintaHealingArts.com

ISBN: 978-1-77277-345-3

Warning – Disclaimer
The purpose of this book is to educate and entertain. The author and/or publisher do not guarantee that anyone following these techniques, suggestions, tips, ideas, or strategies will become successful. The author and/or publisher shall have neither liability nor responsibility to anyone with respect to any loss or damage caused, or alleged to be caused, directly or indirectly by the information contained in this book.

Publisher
10-10-10 Publishing
Markham, ON
Canada

Printed in Canada and the United States of America

Table of Contents

Acknowledgements

Special thanks to my dear and beloved son, Keith, who has been my pride and joy. I call him my miracle. I am here today because of you. You are the one who kept me continuing with my life's journey to find myself, and to be strong and be the person I am today. Having you in my life motivated me to never give up the fight, because I have you to live for. You are the biggest part of my life. I am so blessed to have an exceptionally respectful, and also well respected, son.

Enormous gratitude to my sister, Agnes, for being that very special sister anyone would wish to have, for being my biggest support, for taking care of me in every step of the way, through my health challenges and life challenges, for believing in me, and for being a big part of my life in a big way. You are one person that I know I can truly count on. Your love gave me the strength to overcome many obstacles and challenges I faced in life. You are also my very best friend; you have patience and unconditional love for everyone, which has rubbed off on me, and for which I am truly grateful for. Thank you for putting up with me when I am having a rough day, and for patiently waiting for the storm to pass. We always have great times together, and it amazes everyone when they see how close a bond we have.

I would like to thank my siblings for all of their support and encouragement throughout my life, growing up together and sharing our interest in continuously learning new skills. We are a family that was never afraid of any challenges set before us. You have always been there at every turn in my life, had faith in me in all of my talents, and encouraged me to reach for the stars.

I deeply appreciate my friends, Alaina and Lyndon, for being true and special friends that I am so fortunate to have in my life. You have always been there for me whenever I needed you. Thank you for teaching me that I must also learn to receive, which had been the most difficult thing for me to overcome because I am always ready to help others. You both have always, always been there for me in every way possible. Words cannot express my gratitude for our friendship.

Anne-Marie Henzel, my client/friend, thank you for your support and total trust and confidence in me and my healing gift, to do the healing journey with me. Through this period, we have developed a deep friendship, which I will always cherish; Thank you for your support and help with my mission to help the homeless and less fortunate. Most of all, thank you for giving me the push forward to get my book done.

I am grateful to Craig Grudz, owner of DT Floral and Decor, who had booked my services as a floral designer and holistic practitioner. I have known him for over a decade. Thank you, Craig, for your friendship, and for considering me as a sister. In all the years you have known me, I have always wanted to continue to expand my education and skills. You have always had faith in me and have been supportive and encouraging in everything I put my mind to. You have always believed in me, and that I can achieve anything.

Lili Roman-Thut, you are a client who became a very close, dear, and trusted friend, and it is a friendship I am truly blessed to have. Sometimes I feel you are my biggest fan. You are truly a beautiful person, inside and out. Honesty bleeds through you, which is what I really appreciate in our friendship. You always believe in me and are always so encouraging, and you always remind me of my abilities so that I will continue to shine.

I am unable to name everyone in my life here, but I am so thankful to you all, for your love, support, and encouragement that you have shown me, and for always having faith in me and my abilities. I know

Acknowledgements

I would not be where I am today without each person that is in my life. Thank you for being who you are, and for playing that special role in my life to make it better.

I would like to thank Debra Dsouza, Melissa Cline Taylor, and Mayor Margaret Quirk for personally welcoming me and helping me to make Keswick my new home. Being in this beautiful town made me feel at home and also gave me the motivation to follow my passion and achieve it.

I would also like to thank Krista Tucci. I have come to admire and highly respect you for your friendship, and I am really grateful for your help and guidance with some details I needed to bring my book to fruition.

Foreword

Are you suffering? Have you lost yourself? Is your joy gone? Do people, fears and obstacles dictate your life? Are you stuck and uncertain on how to move forward? Author Jacinta Yang overcomes these familiar challenges and discovers that happiness comes from making your own choices, not from others making them for you. Her story takes you on the journey that challenged her beliefs and gave her the courage to reclaim her life. It will unveil moments that you can relate to, that will help you build curiosity to embrace your change and emerge healthier, stronger and more confident.

In *Take Charge: Reclaim Your Life and Be Your True Self*, Jacinta shares her personal story of overcoming unhealthy relationships, divorce, being alone, health challenges and getting through hard times of uncertainties and doubts. Life was dark and messy. There was self-blame and fear. Thoughts of "how do I get out?" and change were scary for Jacinta as she let go of her familiar life of certainty and comfort. However, Jacinta aspired for change, and to be something different. She discovered that what she learned early in life could be challenged and unlearned. She shifted her thinking and behaviors to embark on a new path and an enlightened mindset.

On the path to pleasure you will go through pain and suffering. Suffering and challenges are essential to growth. You don't grow when life is good. You grow when times are hard. Jacinta found a new kind of personal power to overcome her obstacles and fears, and she used this power to rebuild her life without blaming herself and others. She gained strength from her challenges, experiences and people who were there to support her, and discovered that her suffering diminished. Her creativity and joy emerged, and she has changed how she walks in the world. She transformed her life to reveal her personal healing passion and her hidden super-power.

Jacinta is now in charge of her life. She moves towards what brings her joy. She has found her super-power as a holistic healer using the healing methodologies in Reiki, Reflexology, Crystal Healing and Past Life Regression therapies. Her passion is to help heal you, and take you on a journey of enlightenment and self-discovery. She is passionate about elevating her healing to the next level. She is ready to take on new challenges as they come. She believes that no matter what curve ball life may throw at you, you should not be afraid to tackle it, for you always have a choice to find a solution to handle it.

If you are considering any of these questions, Jacinta's story makes taking charge of your life attainable. It will liberate you to face your fears and overcome your obstacles, change and challenge your thinking, encourage your curiosity, learn and discover your own personal super-power to reclaim your life and be your true-self. Her story will inspire you and propel you forward to ease your suffering, reclaim your life, and move towards a path of joy and purpose.

Life is all about choices and having the courage to make your own. You decide what you want for yourself in life. Jacinta's story to peace and happiness will take you down the roads of love, forgiveness, sharing, caring, faith, hope, courage, and determination. Enjoy your journey and the view along the way.

Raymond Aaron
New York Times Bestselling Author

Chapter 1

Understanding My Life

Reclaiming My Life

You are probably wondering what I mean by "reclaiming my life." You may even be wondering how you reclaim your life when your life is really your own. Yes, my life is mine, so why do I need to reclaim my life? When I say my life is my own, it's actually quite complex, even though it sounds pretty simple.

I first started my life when I was born. However, as a baby, I lived—I existed. Living and existing is not really "living a life." As an infant, it is obvious that I was not really aware of life. At that time, I don't think I could even say that I even knew that I had a life.

During the initial stages of my life, since I was not aware of what life really was, I was dependent on my parents or elders or caregivers for my existence. I needed them to feed me and take care of all my basic needs for my existence.

The first few years of my life, it was obvious that I was dependent on my parents to teach me how to walk, how to talk, how to feed myself, and to be capable of my basic needs.

At this stage, I merely existed and lived the life that was expected of me by my parents. I didn't know any better; therefore, whatever my parents expected of me, I did. This is what I would call the learning stage of my own existence.

The next stage in life was when I started school. The dynamics of my life changed. Now I started to live my life by following the rules and regulations of the school, when I was in school. I followed the rules and regulations of my parents when I was at home. The time I started, school was a learning stage, a different learning stage. The stage of what I learnt in school was more than what I learnt at home, which was basic living skills. This was the stage when I first started to get my education.

Now, as a child in a primary grade, I started to learn how to read and write, and how to interact with other children. I learned to obey my teachers and my elders. I also learnt that there are consequences for disobedience. Back in the day, consequences were pretty severe. Punishment was the norm, over many things. It felt like I could get punished even if I just thought of disobeying any rules.

Fear of punishment was practically drummed into my head, over and over, so that I dared not even think of breaking any rules, or remotely think of being disobedient, be it at home or in school. Punishment was considered a compulsory requirement to discipline—a necessary evil to form character back in the day.

Parents and people in an authoritative role took pride in their harsh disciplinary actions, which could be termed as cruel in this day and age. The harsher the role they played, the more they were respected. People did take pride in their strict and harsh disciplinary ways.

The college I went to was the college of choice, because at the admissions day, the school's strict rules and regulations were laid out as one of Fort Knox, and the professors were presented as some kind of prison wardens—any kind of misbehavior could be a reason for expulsion from the school.

Being a co-ed school, and in an Islamic country, socializing between male and female students was not allowed. With all these strict rules in place, it was considered to be the college I was to attend.

When Did My Life Start?

My life literally began when my parents united and combined two key ingredients to create a life. My life started the day I was conceived, like having different colors to start a painting.

Technically, you could say that I came with a blank canvas, since I came into this world being a child and having absolutely no idea of what life was truly about. I depended on my parents to show me and teach me the basics of painting—basically how to live, and how to live a life of existence. They started to teach me the basic colors.

As time progressed, they taught me how to mix the colors to blend colors; then they taught me how to start painting, i.e. how to function in this world. Later, they taught me how to blend more colors.

Now the painting began, which means that they started to show me or mold me to be the person they wanted me to be. That is when they started to paint the picture on my canvas, painting a picture of a vision they had in their head.

As my parents began to paint the picture, everything seemed fine and beautiful, because I did not know any better. At this point, I didn't have a preference, I didn't have an opinion, and I didn't know any better.

As I got older, I began to learn more about myself. I learnt that I have a preference, as I was more aware of who I was, what I liked and didn't like, what I wanted and didn't want, and what I liked and didn't like to do. That's when I started to realize that I didn't like the picture on the canvas that my parents had painted. It did not suit me. Many of the details didn't resonate with me, and I was not happy because it did not represent me. I began to question myself: Is this the picture I want for myself—the one that my parents painted for me? Or do I prefer to paint my picture myself? I want to live my own life, make my own mistakes, and learn from my own experiences, and be who I want to be.

Who Am I?

Who am I? This is a question that you have probably asked yourself. Did I ask this question when I was young? Certainly not; how could I have asked this question? I couldn't have, because I didn't even know that I was living a life designed for me by my parents. I was just merely existing.

As I grew older, I started to realize that my opinions and choices, and outlook on life, were totally different from that of my family—mainly my parents, but also that of my peers and society.

This is when I questioned everything about the rules and regulations imposed upon me by my family or anyone in authority.

I started to question whether any of these rules and regulations and expectations placed upon me made any sense. If not, then why not? As you can imagine by now, I have started to live in my head a lot. I started to question and analyse everything, to the point that I got into a habit of analysing everything to death, and I was even told that I would analyse things to the minute atom or more if I could.

For generations, people have followed rules and regulations initiated or influenced by traditions and cultures. No one had the courage to question their elders. Lives were lived by many without questioning the logic behind the rules and expectations placed upon them.

People in past generations tended to live their lives based on the expectations of family and society. Society did in fact dictate the lives of many, especially those in public positions.

People born into some families were doomed from the moment they were born, because their lives were already mapped out for them. They were educated and trained to be fit for their position in society. Their personal preferences were not considered to be of any importance.

However, in recent years, there seems to be some changes to this restrictive imposition of what is expected. I didn't know who I was at that time in my life. I was still learning about life.

I was existing in a life dictated by others; so, in some ways, we could say that I did not have an identity. I was the daughter of so and so, and the sister of so and so. My identity did not matter because I was supposed to be an obedient child to my parents and older siblings; it was of utmost importance to have respect for the elders, without question.

I was not to have an opinion; if I did, it did not matter. I was to remain silent if my opinion was not the same as my elders. Freedom of expression was not accepted if it was contradictory.

I had to obey everything that was expected of me, so to even entertain the thought of having my own thoughts, was unacceptable. Therefore, how was I to know at this point in my life who I even was?

I do not recall if it even crossed my mind at the time to even think that I needed to know who I was, or what it was that I wanted out of my life. I did not even remotely imagine that the need to really know who I was, was really important.

I was not allowed to question, for any reason, whatever we were instructed to do. The answer would be, "Because I said so, and you will do as you are told." I am sure that many of you can relate to this famous terminology, if you happen to be from the same era as myself.

I am sure that there are still some cultures to this day that have the same dynamics, but with the outside influences, it's not as rigidly implemented as it was in the past. People are learning to have a voice.

Was I Living My Life?

Was I living my life? This was a question that did not occur for many years of my life, because I was not aware that I was not really living a life of my own. I lived a life; yes, I did. As previously stated, I lived a life designed by my parents or elders.

What do I mean by "living my life?" When I say "living my life as my own," I am talking about a life of my own choice—a life where I make my own decisions, make my own choices, make my own mistakes, and suffer the consequences of the choices or decisions I make, and not suffer the consequences of a choice or decisions made for me.

I was raised by a family that was extremely strict—in my own personal opinion, a family that was overly protective. Also, being of a strict Catholic background, the chances of me living a life of my own was highly unlikely, to practically non-existent.

I went to school, came home, and did activities with my siblings around the home, or I worked alongside my siblings in the family's home-based business. In my early years, my siblings and I were not allowed to play with the neighbor's children, as we were not allowed to leave our home.

I was not allowed to go on school trips without a written request from the teacher, and a guarantee that the teacher would be at my side at all times. I was not allowed to go to my classmates' or friends' birthday parties. However, I was allowed to invite friends or classmates over to our home. A sleepover at a friend's home was absolutely out of the question. We dared not even dream of asking for permission.

Living under such circumstances, I could definitely say that any hope or wish to live a life of my own, at a young age, was clearly unimaginable. I couldn't even fathom the possibility to do so. Plus, at this stage, I was still unaware that I could if I truly wanted to; after all, I was still dependent on my parents or elders to make decisions for me, and to help me with my basic needs in life.

My life belonged to my parents, to do as they wished and as they designed. They decided what school I was to attend, what school major I should take, and what career path I was to have. I am sure some of you can relate to this scenario, as it was a common pattern for those of us born back in my time.

I am sure this pattern still exists to this day in some cultures, as it's common in some cultures to have such family dynamics. I would say that this is common in Eastern cultures, even though things have advanced a lot with the influence from the West. However, I am also aware of some families even in the Western cultures.

There are still some parents that do have similar expectations of the children to this present day, so I really do not want to make any generalizations. So, in reality, some of us are not immune to this family dynamic, no matter which culture we are born into, or which part of the world we are in.

Therefore, given that such a family dynamic is in existence, it is difficult for a person in their initial stage of life to be able to have the freedom to be their true self. To become our true selves, no matter what society or family dynamics we are born into, we have to go through a personal journey to find ourselves—to examine who we are and what we are all about—to be really aware of who we are before we can really be our true selves.

Did I Know If My Life Was Mine?

I was most certainly not living a life of my own, since I was not even aware of the fact that I was not even living a life of my own. I lived where I existed. Life carried on from day to day.

From childhood to my teenage years, my life was all about going to school, like you and everyone else in the world.

First, I received my primary education, and then as I advanced to my teenage years or adulthood, plans were made for me, and a decision was made for me as to what field or profession I should consider for my future. A few generations ago, it was common that professions were passed down from generation to generation.

My father followed in the footsteps of his father and became a cobbler. However, my brother did not follow in my father's field. He decided to go a different route.

As for myself, being the youngest child, and also going to college at a very young age of 15 years, it was decided for me that I was to go into the commerce field, since there really were not many options available to me. In fact, there really were not many options open for the students at all.

My interest and passion was more on the arts or the creative side, but there were no courses available that suited my interests. Also, my mother believed that artists only become famous and rich after they have passed from this earth. I possess strong mathematical skills and am a logical person, so the best choice was in commerce and accounting. I proceeded to go to college to acquire my Intermediate Commerce and Bachelor of Commerce Degree.

Keeping that in mind, it was obvious that I did not live my life on my own during my childhood years, nor in my youth. This of course carries throughout my life as a college student.

In college, my life was dictated by the principal or the professors. We learnt what we were taught. Being a good student, I naturally followed all the rules and regulations of the college, or I would be punished. We were threatened to be expelled if we did not abide by the rules and regulations of the college.

Being expelled was considered to be the most shameful experience for any student and their family; therefore, no students, nor myself, would even dare to think of challenging the college rules.

Meanwhile, in the home setting, I worked in our family restaurant; and like most people, as well as my own siblings, I did as I was expected to by my parents—school during the day, and work after school. Working in a restaurant, as you may already know, is a long day every day. Such circumstances simply did not allow me to have time to even think of myself or for myself. I was on daily autopilot.

I feel certain that many people lived their lives in such a manner. Many people are in autopilot mode and could easily spend the rest of their lives fulfilling the expectations of others, and are never even aware of their circumstances. I consider this as living a life while sleeping or unaware; hence, the term, *unawakened one*.

In recent years, I feel that more and more people are starting to awaken, and they are thus questioning themselves on who they are and what they are all about, and are also in search of their life purpose. Less and less people are now settling to live a life on autopilot. They want to have a meaning to their life, and make a difference in this world.

Why Was I Not Living My Life?

Life is such a complex topic; we have so many questions that can revolve around it, and trying to answer them is also just as complex.

Where do we even begin? I have already covered a few questions, such as what is life, and when did my life begin? Who am I in the circle of life? Am I living my life? Am I not living my life? Now my question is, why was I not living my life? Even though the question is so closely related, there are some subtle changes to it.

Now to really get to the point of why I was not living my own life.

There are so many factors as to why I was not living my life. First and foremost, when we really get into the nitty gritty part of it all, I came into this world as a baby—a living, breathing being—with absolutely no knowledge of how to really feed myself or even really function.

I depended on my parents to teach me all the absolute basics; therefore, as a baby, to live my life as my own was out of the question.

As a toddler, I still depended on my parents or other family members for their guidance of life's daily activities: how to identify things in my immediate surrounding, how to keep safe from things and what to avoid, learning to speak and communicate for my basic needs, or learning basic activities, such as learning to walk so that I could be somewhat independent and a bit more mobile.

As I grew older and learnt to be more independent physically, and to have the ability to function with daily activities and to go to school for education, this still did not qualify me to be able to live a life of my own.

I was not qualified to live a life of my own yet, as I had not yet gained enough experience or knowledge to really know how to live a life that

I could truly call my own; I was still not aware of myself, or of what I liked or did not like for certain. I was still learning what I had a preference for, as well as what resonated or did not resonate with me. These were some of the reasons why I was not living a life of my own.

To really be living a life of my own or be who I really am, it was important that I must first have the awareness of who I am. What am I all about? In order for me to be aware, I needed to go through some life experiences in order to have the knowledge and to know more about myself, and what it was that I wanted out of life. Who did I want to be? What did I want to do with my life?

All of these questions can only be answered by having lived and gone through life experiences. It is the challenges that life throws at us that give us the experiences to become aware of our nature, our personality traits, our inner beliefs, and our inner calling, or what I would call our core self, or what some may even call our soul.

When we understand that we have a soul, and we know what our soul is all about, I think it is then that we are able to know who we are and what kind of life we want to live. Only then can we proceed to learn to live a life of our own.

I need to go through this whole process in order for me to begin to understand why I was not living a life of my own.

Chapter 2

The Life I Was Living

Did I Know That My Life Was Not Mine?

How many of us go through life, like myself, and are not aware that we are living a life that does not feel like our own? Did I know that my life was truly mine?

I did not know that my life was not truly mine, which is why I lived the life that was designed for me. I went to the school chosen for me. I did everything that was expected of me. It almost felt like I lived and breathed as I was told, day in and day out.

Actually, it is not true that it felt like so, but in fact, it was pretty much the reality of my life while living at home with my family. Then my marriage was arranged; I got engaged at the young age of 21 years, and I was married by the time I turned 22 years old. At that young age, having lived a very sheltered life with no exposure to the outside world, I was still living in the dark; hence, I was unaware of the fact that I was living a life that I would not consider my own.

I was married to a man who was very insecure and controlling, and not knowing any better, I carried on living and catering to the wishes of my husband and his family. I did not matter, and I practically did not exist other than the fact that I was a slave to the family, and a punching bag for my husband's verbal frustration.

According to him, I could not be a friend; I was a wife, on whom he could dump his frustrations of his day. I felt like I was trapped in a prison of my husband's making. He imposed his rule on me: "Facts of life are no compromise." I cannot consider that I could expect him to compromise with me for anything. I had no rights or expectations of any of my wishes.

I was not even allowed to invite my best friend to my own wedding. It was therefore obvious that at this stage of my life, I did not know that my life was mine, and that was why I lived and endured the life I was living, without question.

The more I lived this life—the experience of feeling miserable daily and being emotionally abused by my husband and his family—it made me become more aware of what I did not want for myself, and this was when I started to feel that this was not a life that I wanted for myself.

I felt trapped and like a prisoner. Even though I was not actually trapped in a prison cell, I was trapped in a much stronger prison cell. The prison cell was the fear of breaking free from this life, the fear of how people would view me as a person, and how my family would react to my breaking free.

On a daily basis, these fears prevented me from breaking free from the prison that I was living in. Fear prevented me from thinking for myself. It was the same fear that prevented me from knowing much beyond myself; I was engulfed by fear that kept me in the dark for years.

Being in the dark, it was really difficult to see anything else. I was not able to see any possibilities of anything else. The fear also handicapped me from taking action, because fear shows an ugly face an ugly outcome, which ultimately prevented me from taking any action.

When fear engulfed my mind, I definitely was not aware at that time that my life was really mine. I don't think I even knew what that term meant.

The Life I Was Living Was Not Mine

Being born and raised in Pakistan, a country where it is the norm for everyone to live their lives according to family wishes and pressure from society, did not help much.

I was living a life that was expected of me by my family; plus, the whole entire society had the same outlook on life. With this in mind, it was very natural for me to think that this was the norm. Many people that I knew lived a very similar life, governed by family and society; therefore, it was very easy to be in the dark that my life was not mine. It did not even cross my mind that the life I was living wasn't even remotely close to how I wanted to live my life as my own.

Since I was not aware at this stage that this was not normal or even acceptable, I went from one prison to the next, i.e. from my family setting to that of my husband and his family.

Being young and naive, I didn't have enough experience in life to know that the life I was living was not mine. I did not really choose the life I was living. It was chosen for me. Was I at fault? Had I known better, or was I aware that I had a right to my life? Yes, I would be at fault, but since I was not yet aware at the time, then I would say that I was merely living like a robot.

This robot was programmed to follow instructions. First, I was programmed by my family; then when I was handed over to my husband, I was reprogrammed to follow new sets of instructions.

Living in an abusive marriage, I started to question life, my life, and what I was living with and how unhappy I was. I began to pay attention to my daily life and what I was going through. That was when I did in fact question life, and whether I had a right to my life.

As mentioned earlier, living in fear kept me in the dark. I was too unhappy at the time to be able to think clearly. I didn't have any support, and I lived in my own world in my head, not having much knowledge of what was available outside of my trapped world, or that there were so many possibilities.

It was not common practice for most to openly share anything personal, so I felt ashamed to do so when thinking of sharing what I was going through in my life. It was too embarrassing a thought to consider exposing my personal life. Then there was a matter of self-blame. I knew I was a person of determination, which was considered to be a stubborn trait that was looked down upon.

You will notice that I may talk a lot about fear, and how fear blocks us in many areas of our lives. Fear has many faces, and I will expose the different faces of fear that I encountered in my life, as I proceed further into the following chapters.

Here, I would say that the fear of being judged prevented me from knowing that the life I was living was not mine. I can pretty well guarantee that everyone in the world does face some sort of fear in their life. I learnt that I did indeed have some fears, even though in many ways I was fearless. Yet I realized that there were other areas of my life in which I had fears, and the willingness to admit that I did in fact have some fear was the first step for me to go within, in search of all of my fears and weaknesses.

Before I knew I had fears, I really did not know much about myself; hence, I did not know that I was not living my life. There is a saying: "When you don't know what you don't know, that's when you actually have a problem."

How Did I Live Then?

When I was pregnant with my son, I went through a very rough pregnancy, and I was not really sure why. It is quite possible that I was not in a very good mental state due to the emotional abuse I was going through from my husband and his family.

I was in hospital for throwing up constantly. The morning sickness started early in the pregnancy, and it continued through my entire pregnancy. I was at risk, 24/7, of losing my baby, and I was also kept in hospital on 24-hour Gravol anti-nausea medication, intravenously, which did not stop the nausea. When I was discharged, I was assigned a public health nurse to monitor my health during my pregnancy.

The emotional abuse, from my husband and his family who lived with us (his parents and 2 brothers), was a daily routine as I struggled through my pregnancy. Finally, my beautiful baby boy was born. It was the happiest day of my life, even to this day.

After my son was born, the nurse was ready to discharge me, but when she realized that I was in an abusive situation, she decided to postpone the discharge.

After giving birth to my son, and living in an abusive relationship (which at the time I thought was a normal way of life), I lost interest in having an intimate relationship, which I also thought was normal after childbirth. I announced that I had decided to give up intimate relations for the rest of my life.

That announcement did not go over too well with my husband. The verbal abuse became more magnified. The daily rape now began, and I did not even know that a husband could rape his wife. Silently, I endured my fate. I put on a smile daily and went to work. I was very good at hiding the life I lived. I was ashamed and embarrassed to talk to anyone about my life.

I reached out to the nurse that had been assigned to me during my pregnancy, to inquire if childbirth could be the reason for my lack of interest in having an intimate relationship. She did not give me an answer, but rather she decided to visit me at my place of work to talk to me. In hindsight, I realize now why she chose to do that.

She was aware that I was living with an abusive family, and chose not to visit me at home. She also knew that I was very unaware of many things in life. She chose to let me talk about my daily life and daily routine, for weeks, and then I finally realized through my venting that I was a person and not a piece of meat, and that I should be treated like a person and be respected.

I do not recall how many weeks she visited me at work so that I could just talk and vent. With the first realization, she referred me to a doctor, who in turn referred me to a social worker with whom I could have a weekly visit. I attempted to request my husband to go with me so that we could discuss our issues and perhaps resolve them.

His response was, "I am not crazy, and I don't need to see a counsellor." I didn't realize that he had been warned by his co-worker that all such visits are documented and that he should avoid them. He often forbade me to spend time with my family, for fear that I may reveal his abusive nature. He collected my pay cheque the moment I walked in the door on pay day.

I dreaded to go home every day, not knowing what I was going to face that day, but I knew for sure that it was not going to be pleasant. I could practically hear my mother-in- law's loud demanding voice from a block away. I would cringe at the thought of my evenings and nights. I was living in my own dark world, and that is how I lived.

When Did I First Realize That My Life Was Mine?

During my conversation with the public health nurse, who helped me dig deep inside of me for the answers I was seeking, I began to figure out that after all of those years, I was merely living a life that was imposed upon me. I started to think and wonder how I did not know that.

With my regular visits with my social worker, I learnt even more that the life I was living was one that was abused. None of what I was living with or putting up with was acceptable. I was informed of the fact that a husband does not have the right to rape his wife.

With this new knowledge, I informed my spouse that it was not acceptable for a husband to rape his wife. He ignored the information he had just learnt, and he continued his daily/nightly routine. One fine morning, I pleaded through my tears for him to stop. He did, and he said, "Remember Father's Day 1990? I did not rape you."

Through my visits with the social worker, I learnt a lot about myself, my rights, and my role in this world, as I continued to learn more of the outside world—the world outside of my family and my spouse's family, in Canada now instead of Pakistan—where society is completely different, and where women have more rights, and social norms are different.

Learning about what is socially or morally accepted here in Canada was a big relief for me, because I think I am by nature a strong willed and free spirit. I felt restricted all my life, and I learned that being a strong willed and free spirit is in fact a very positive trait to have, and is not to be suppressed.

All the knowledge I gained from my weekly visits helped me to realize that my life was indeed my own, to live as I please and want, and not how my family or others want. So my life is mine—now what?

I began to analyze the life I was living, and I started to think and examine myself as well, trying to learn more about myself and what it was that I believed in. What did I want out of life?

I was now on a mission to learn about myself, so I started to pay close attention to everything in my life now. My need to understand myself and my life got stronger as time progressed, and that was when I realized that there were some fears I had that needed to be addressed in order for me to be able to take the step to learn more and more about myself.

I started to feel that I was slowly coming out of the darkness I was living in, and as some light started to shine in bit by bit, that was how I started to know that I am an individual that is entitled to be my own person, and that my life is truly mine. I have the right to live it as I please, and no one has the right to control my life or dictate how I should live it.

I would like everyone who is reading this to remember that you are your own person— your life is yours, you have the right to live it as you please and as you wish, and no one has the right or authority to tell you how to live it. If you wish to live it according to someone else's wishes, it should be your choice if you wish to do so, if that would make you happy.

There are some people who choose to live by someone else's wishes because they prefer to do so, as they feel they are happier when they are following someone else's wishes because it's easier for them. They feel that they like to be guided by someone for different reasons; as in some cases, they prefer to leave the responsibility to others, to make decisions for them, and that is perfectly fine if it's their own choice.

When Did I Begin to Live My Life?

In my 20s, after having lived a very sheltered life, as well as a life that was controlled by others for over two decades, I had learned little about what life is really about and how I own my life. It was very new to me; so, now my journey begins.

Learning about myself, and who I really am, did take some time and processing—after all, the true and real me had been suppressed practically from the time I was born. In order to really learn and understand myself, it certainly and definitely took interactions with people that I came in contact with. Interaction with others was what gave me the awareness of what my inner core being was.

Even though I may have come to the realization that my life is my own, it was not easy to just start to live it as I pleased, since I was conditioned to live a certain way. There were many factors that contributed to my inability to start living as I pleased: the fear of the unknown, of what was in store for me, and whether I should start to live as I pleased or continue to live as conditioned.

I may now have realized that my life is my own, but to break from the cycle of the life of being controlled was not easy, because fear prevented me from doing so. As a child, I was pretty fearless in many ways. I often thought that I was fearless, but if I were to examine myself in different areas of my life, I would have to be honest and say that I am not all that fearless, as I thought myself to be.

I never knew that I had fear. Because of my lack of fear in other areas of my life, people that I knew would see me as a strong, fearless person.

I gave a different name to the fear that I felt within. Yes, I do admit that I did have fear: fear of how my actions would affect people I cared about, and fear about what people would think of me. Would I be judged for my behavior? Would I be considered a cold person for having a mind of my own?

So much went through my head the more I thought about my life, myself, and the possible consequences of my possible actions that I may take. That was how I started to recognize the many faces of fear as mentioned above. It certainly was a huge revelation for me that I wasn't all that fearless after all, as I had thought myself to be.

I was fearless, yes, but only in a minute area of my life when I come to think of it. Having this revelation about myself didn't feel good to me. I did not like the knowledge that I was being fearful or weak, and I did not feel good about myself. Having known this for the first time, I would say that put me into a situational depression, because situational depression is really self-directed anger.

I was angry at myself for being weak and fearful, and for allowing all these fears to prevent me from facing those challenges in my life, and I mindlessly allowed the doctor to put me on medication for depression. The side effects of the medication started to make me feel sluggish and to not think clearly. It did not make me happy that I was feeling that I had lost the ability to think.

I felt it was very important for me to be mentally alert and have the ability to think clearly, if I was going to get myself out of the dilemma I was in, living a controlled life. I consulted with my doctor that I did not wish to continue the medication, since we were both aware that I was suffering from situational depression. I felt that if I could correct my situation, then I would get myself out of the depression I was suffering from.

The doctor agreed that I was making the right decision, and began working on solutions to help get me out of the depression I was in.

How Do I Go About Living My Life?

Living a life of my own wasn't exactly an easy process. There was still so much to learn about life and about myself. It was like starting a brand new painting. I needed to prepare a canvas, and different colored paints and paint brushes all needed to be carefully chosen and planned. A vision was also needed so that a picture could be painted.

Still being married at this stage, and still living under the control of my husband, only now with a new set of eyes, and knowledge that I have a choice, made me question many actions and behaviors of the family members in regard to how I was being treated—was it acceptable to me? I made excuses for their behavior; I tried to justify it.

Then there was the matter of my religion. Being raised as a Catholic and going to a Catholic school, I had learnt that we must be obedient, make sacrifices, endure hardships, etc. With all of these ingrained in my head at an early age, I was not too clear on what was truly expected of me by my creator. I tried to be a good Catholic, so I thought that I needed to make sacrifices—sacrifice what makes me happy, and endure the abuse that I was living in.

I felt anger every day, and then I would feel that I was committing a sin, since anger is a sin. I went to church to confess my sin and ask for forgiveness for my daily anger. I went to confess to the priest my sin of anger that I felt I committed every day. The priest felt the need for more details, so he requested that I have a meeting with him at his office.

After the meeting, he understood my reasons. He then assured me that God did not mean for me to suffer the way I was suffering. He assured me that I was doing my best and that the situation I was living in was not what God wanted me to be in. I must learn to take care of myself. So here I am now with a new realization—that even God does not accept the abuse inflicted upon me in my marriage. With this new knowledge, there was more to think about, yet life continued as before.

I was learning more and more about how the life I was living at the time was really not an acceptable one. It was not acceptable to God, and it was not acceptable to this new society that I was living in.

All this knowledge led me to dive deeper within to try to find answers for myself as to what I must do. I needed answers. After a great deal of thought, I concluded that I needed to get myself out of my depression. To get out of my depression, I must stop being angry at myself for being weak. In order for me to stop being angry at myself for being weak, it was necessary for me to face the many ugly faces of fear.

In order to do that, I needed to determine what all those fears were that were stopping me from moving forward. I then proceeded to examine each fear one by one, and I tried to find a solution for every fear that was being a handicap and preventing me from moving forward.

It was not easy to overcome it, but it was necessary for me to face it if I was to free myself from the prison that I allowed myself to be in. I mustered up every ounce of courage I could possibly find within myself, and I faced one fear at a time to move on to the next step towards my road to freedom.

It was a painful process because I had no support of any kind, but I felt it was a necessary step that I must take in order for me to open the door to my freedom—the freedom to choose how I want to live, and the person I want to be.

Chapter 3

Self-Realization

Who Am I Now?

I am asking myself again: Who am I? Who am I now? Yes, I ask this question again, because I am still in search of myself, and learning about me. It is a bit difficult because I am still learning about life. It is such a slow process because my contact with the outside world had been so limited. I had been restricted to limited contact, by my former husband, and if I had any contact at all, it was with objections and unpleasant outcomes.

As my visits to the social worker were regular despite the objections, I found it to be helpful for me as I learnt a lot about social acceptance of what I was dealing with at home. The more knowledge I gained in this area, the more confidence I gained, and the fearless traits that I had within started to surface, bit by bit. I learnt to speak up, and I started to gain some voice.

However, that was not quite enough to set me free from the controlled life I was living. I still endured the daily abuse, as I still did not have the strength as of yet. However, I must say, at least I was no longer living in total darkness; or rather, I was no longer clueless to the life I was living.

I was totally aware at this point that I was very unhappy with my life; I was unhappy that I was not respected or appreciated. My efforts of being a good wife or daughter-in-law were totally unacknowledged and unappreciated.

I am now still trying to find myself, because the fear I lived with, and the kind of life I was living, made it a bit difficult. Every day, I wanted the day to be over. The only way it was going to be over was to try not to have too many conflicts, go to work, do chores, and spend hours in the day with detailed cleaning of the house, so that I would be too tired to even think and deal with the nightly fate.

Even though I tried to numb my daily abuse, the only positive thing for me was that I was no longer clueless as I had been before. Through my daily trauma, I had a sharp mind that helped me think things through, and I would go over these things and try to find solutions to the problems I was living with.

First, I tried to have a decent conversation by making a rational request that I be treated with respect or as a friend, or that we should, as husband and wife, make compromises. His response was, "You are my wife, and you are supposed to take all the crap I need to unload. The fact of life is that there is no compromise."

All of this made it very evident that I had no hope in hell to be treated with respect, or to be viewed as an equal with whom he was sharing his life. I was treated like a slave, a nursemaid to his paraplegic mother, and a person who brought in a pay cheque, only to hand it over as soon as I walked in the door on payday.

My wallet was to be inspected to make sure I had no funds; then he would make fun of me, saying, "I did not know my wife is so poor that she does not even have a cent in her wallet." However, I did have a credit card, which was secondary to his, so I really did not even have a credit history of my own.

So really, at this point, who was I really? I was still the same person who was clueless, someone who was currently confused as to who I was now, and I knew that I was not someone who wanted to have my life controlled by others—yet I still was. I think I can safely say that who I really am now is someone who is slowly learning to grow wings, and slowly finding a way to take my life back.

Do I Own My Life Yet?

Yes, I do ask myself now if I do in fact own my life yet. Finding a way to take my life back was not an easy task. My knowledge about myself and the world surrounding me, and about what is acceptable and what is not acceptable, was indeed the biggest factor that helped me to examine the life I was living.

Learning about what was important to me as to how I liked to be treated was the key factor in learning my own self-worth. I began to learn that I have my own personal goals and wishes and dreams that I wish to fulfill. But since I was restricted from realizing my dreams and goals, I guess I would say that I still did not own my own life.

How would I do that? I still did not know. But one thing I did know was that I did not intend to live the life I was living. The main reason I did not want to live this life was because I have a son who depends on me. I did not want to have him see the daily abuse that I was living with. He was barely two, but he knew that something was not right; he presented protective behavior towards me.

It was his protective behavior towards me that tore at my heart—I should be the one protecting him, not the other way around. The thought of my role as an adult to be the protector, was what gave me the courage to seriously think. I had to seriously think of how not to continue this way of life much longer, as I did not wish for my son to have too many memories of the life I lived before his very eyes.

This was the biggest turning point for me to take matters into my own hands, and to seriously consider finding solutions to take charge of my own life. It was important for my son's sake that I do. I needed to find the courage to be my own person and to set a good example for him.

My need to be a good mother and a good example for my son, and to be the responsible adult who should be the protective one, is what gave me the courage to start to face my fears and learn to tackle each challenge with courage and strength.

My ability to be logical was the main factor that helped me to overcome my fears one at a time, and that helped me to face them. I now proceeded to teach myself how to overcome my fears as I came face to face with the challenges that I encountered, and with the fears that prevented me from facing and overcoming the challenges in front of me.

When I faced my fears and proceeded to overcome the challenges life threw at me, I began to feel more confident that there was always a solution to all challenges, and that if I did not allow fear to hinder me from moving forward, then nothing and no one could stop me from accomplishing my own goal of being who I wanted to be as a person.

It is therefore important for me to know more about myself and what is within my soul. What kind of person do I truly want to be so that I can look at myself in the mirror and be proud of the reflection in front of me? I know this did not really occur to me on a conscious level, but I am sure that somewhere deep in my subconscious level, I knew that this was what prompted me to proceed with my life as I did.

Our subconscious minds do in fact play a huge role in our lives, even though we are not aware of it. I know that at the time during my growth and transition, I had absolutely no understanding about the subconscious mind, but I am certain, now that I have a better understanding of the subconscious mind, that everyone's lives are definitely affected by the programming of our subconscious minds. Therefore, it is important that we learn how to program our subconscious minds if we wish to achieve certain goals in our lives.

What Should I Do Now?

Having come to a very important awareness, what should I do now? Now that I felt that I needed to do something about the situation and the environment I was living in, it was not really all that simple to do anything about it right away, since there were so many hurdles to overcome—hurdles that I was not yet aware of.

At this point, all I knew was that something had to be done for me to change my circumstances. How and what I had to do to make that happen was still unknown to me, since I was yet to discover more about myself and my own strengths and capabilities. All of this was still buried within me as I was not allowed to be who I really was.

I still felt that I was constricted and needed to learn for myself what steps I needed to take. I felt that I had come to a realization that there was a whole new world on the other side of this big huge boulder and multiple obstacles. There were different size rocks that were blocking the passage to the opening of this new world awaiting me.

My dilemma was how to go about removing the obstacles in front of me in order for me to go through this opening that was available for me to get through. I was now in need of understanding what all these obstacles were, and how to go about removing them so that I could clear a passage for myself.

Some of these rocks were small and easy to pick up and move out of the way; some were heavier and needed more effort to lift them out of the way, while others were impossible to budge.

The next step was to figure out how to move these gigantic boulders that were almost impossible to move, but it was important to remove these big obstacles in order for me to get through.

The big boulders represented a more difficult challenge, and that the solutions were more complicated and needed to be carefully thought out so as to find a proper solution that would help me and not have any negative impact on others. I have always believed deep in my heart that no matter what I do, I do not want my actions to have any negative impact on anyone else.

With that in mind, at times, finding solutions to the problem took time and careful consideration, plus courage to overcome any fears that may show their face to me.

Once I was able to move the large boulders off to the side, to help me to open up a passage to move forward, the smaller obstacles were much easier to move since I had built up the strength to move the large obstacles.

From time to time, I was still faced with difficult challenges, but I learnt that with determination and courage, I would be able to overcome those challenges. In time, I learnt to develop the skills and courage to face everything that life threw at me.

I learnt more about myself through this process. I learnt that I have overcome many fears, and now I am no longer afraid of any challenges I may encounter. This led to me having more confidence in my own abilities and strengths.

What Are the Obstacles I Faced?

I am sure you are probably wondering what these obstacles are that are blocking the passage to my freedom. Living all my life up to this point under someone else's control makes it obvious that I did not have to think for myself, as living that life was like having a map that was already prepared for me, and all I had to do was follow the route already mapped out—all obstacles were already removed, and all I had to do was just go through as directed.

But now that I made the decision to go through this blocked passage, I was really on my own, and I had to clear my own passage. It was like I needed to go through this long tunnel before I could reach the destination I wished to get to. Along the way, the hurdles varied, and I had to tackle them as I went along.

So now back to what you want to know: What were these hurdles? The biggest hurdles to overcome in life were fear, religion, culture, and habits. Smaller hurdles were so small and insignificant that I couldn't even think of what to name them. It was the large hurdles that kept blocking me; at times it even felt like it handicapped me from chipping away this blocker.

I am sure that you can totally relate to what I am talking about with the above hurdles I just mentioned, because I know that you too had to face such hurdles as you encountered them yourself, and you know that it is not that easy to overcome them in some circumstances.

There are also some hurdles that may not be easy to move because there are people involved that are keeping the blocks up. It is like you try to move them away, and then someone keeps placing the blocks back into your path.

At first, you may peacefully remove them without confronting them about keeping the path clear, till you reach a point when you have to firmly inform others to not interfere with your decisions to clear the path for yourself.

That is what I had to do in some circumstances; I had to make sure that there was no one obstructing my path. Family members are generally the ones that may tend to put an obstacle in the path, because they have a different view and opinion as to what my destination is.

They tend to think they know what is better for me, and they try to map out the route for me, but I feel that they do not really understand what my path is or what my destination is, or what destination I wish to reach.

Having differences in opinions and views in my life path or journey, it was necessary for me to continuously try to clear my path each time I felt a blockage was placed before me. I am certain they felt they did not hinder me, but what they did not realize was that by being adamant in their views and opinions on what I should or should not do, it was indeed a blockage for me.

I felt that because I was the youngest in the family, they thought I didn't have the knowledge and experience to know better. They simply did not give me the credit for my intellect and capability to think things through thoroughly before I took actions to the decisions I would make.

They were not aware of my mental capability, nor did they take time to really understand or really get to know me before making assumptions of me. They somehow prejudged me, which created a big obstacle for me to overcome.

Planning Out My Route

Have I planned out my route yet? I can't say that I have just yet, as I am still feeling the need for my freedom to live my life. I am at a confused stage of my life, with very limited knowledge of the outside world. I have now just learnt about a world that exists outside the world I was living in.

My main goal at this time is to imagine what it is like to be free from all the restrictions imposed upon me, and what it feels like to live a life of my own, make my own decisions, and make my own mistakes. It was tough to imagine something that I had no knowledge of, and nothing to compare to.

The first time I was able to remotely relate to something that felt like freedom was when I saw the movie, *Sleeping With the Enemy*. It was in the scene where Julia Roberts planned her escape from her life with her abusive husband. She had just rented a home, and she was standing outside, feeling free at last. Being an empath and seeing the look on her face of feeling free, I felt that moment in the scene. I said to myself, "So this is how it feels to feel free."

I savoured the feeling of that moment and hung on to it like my saving grace, which in fact it was. The feeling of relief was so real, and I needed to make it my reality. Keeping that feeling alive in me, it motivated me to long for the moment that I could experience it for myself in my own reality. Looking back now, I must say that the movie, *Sleeping With the Enemy*, did in fact impact my life in a big way. I even recall bursting out loud in the movie theater, to my husband (who took me to see that movie), "Oh my God, he is just like you."

Day after day, since the movie, I could not help reliving the feeling about feeling free and being on my own. The more I relived it, the more I longed for that freedom. I wanted a life that was not restricted; I wanted to be as free as a bird and fly with my own two wings, feel the wind on my face, and fly high and reach for the stars.

I had so much potential buried within me that needed to come out. I needed to find my own gifts from inside of me. I needed to find me— who am I? What am I all about? Could I find myself?

So many questions started to crop up for me. I spent a lot of time in my head thinking, wondering, and analyzing everything to death so that I could have a better understanding of everything. I had an insatiable need to understand everything. If something did not make sense, I had to wrack my brains till I could understand. I was always searching for answers.

I have always been curious all my life, so it is no surprise to me that I have an insatiable desire to learn and acquire knowledge all the time; therefore, everything has to make sense to me. If it did not, then I needed to make sure that I had an answer that would make sense to me.

I feel that things must make sense to me both mentally and emotionally. For me, emotions and logic must meet somewhere in the middle. Whenever I had to make any decisions, it was important for me to have logic and emotions meet, or else any decision based outside of this would not make sense. And it is possible to regret the decisions made in those circumstances.

Did I Find Myself?

Did I find myself? At that time, I thought I did, but looking back now, I would say that I did not entirely; but I would say that I did find a big part of me. The reason I say that I found a part of me is because it was huge for me to know that I am someone just like you and many other people—I want to be my own person, and I want to be free of being controlled.

There are many people who go through their entire lives searching for themselves. Some may spend an entire lifetime still searching. For me, I think I have known who I was at a fairly young age, at least in part. I would say that I knew who I was; however, some minor part was hidden deep within me, and it needed to come out to shine.

I was at a group meeting, with people that were dealing with family that had cancer. I was in my mid-20s, and a woman commented to the facilitator of the group about me. She said that at such a young age, I already knew who I was. Meanwhile, she was in her late 50s and still trying to find herself. At the time, I would say that I was confident in knowing who I was, but I now would say that I still had a lot to learn about myself.

Self-Realization

You may even be wondering how you go about finding yourself. Like you and me, I believe that most people in the world are, at different times in their lives, asking these very questions: How do I find myself? What do I need to do to find myself?

I believe that people who are moving towards a spiritual journey will definitely ask themselves these very questions, because they are on the quest to understand the meaning of life and their purpose in this world. They are willing to learn and grow; therefore, they will on this journey of self-discovery.

Life is a constant learning school; we are always learning more and more about ourselves every day. I had courage and strength, and I was fearless. I soon learnt that I had the courage to leave my abusive marriage. I did not fear not being able to support myself and start a new life.

I did however soon learn that there were other areas in my life where I did indeed need to overcome some other fears, as well as learn to have the courage to face some challenges.

Courage and fear have so many faces, and with experience, we learn to recognize the various faces and learn. Since there are so many faces to fear and courage, it seems to me that I tend to be repeating myself over and over, but yet if you pay real close attention, you may be able to know that there are some differences.

Did I find myself? At that stage of my life, I believed that I did, but if I were to look at my life then and now, I would say that I did not really find myself entirely back then, but I did find out a lot about myself in comparison to before. I feel that between now and then, I learnt a lot about myself, and I am sure that I will continue to learn more about myself in the future, so that I will find myself even more.

I believe that I am always growing and will always continue to grow, and with new experiences and new challenges that life will continue to throw at me, the only difference is that I am more equipped to face it now than I was in the past.

Chapter 4

Overcoming Obstacles

What Challenges Did I Face to Reclaim My Life?

I can say with certainty that you, I, and everyone on this planet has challenges in life. It is something we definitely cannot escape. Challenges can make life interesting, or they can also destroy a person. Challenges are the very same thing I spoke of as blockages and hurdles. I needed courage and strength to deal with the obstacles and hurdles that life threw at me in my path.

When we say that we are fearless, it ultimately means that we are courageous; yet somehow, I feel there is some difference. I have no idea why, so let us not debate on it. Just ignore me on this because as I write, you may find that I may mention that I had the courage to... or did not fear... I guess I would most likely use the terms that I feel appropriate to express myself.

Strength and courage may be of the same category, yet there is a difference. Strength can mean physical strength as well as emotional and mental strength. Courage is to have the ability to have the strength to overcome fear and proceed.

I have come to realize that in some areas of my life, I seem to naturally lack fear, and thus I have the ability and strength to handle some situations with ease because I am very logical. Being logical was helpful in erasing fear almost instantaneously.

Logic definitely promotes mental strength and helps with emotional strength. Logic helps to keep emotions in check, although when emotions run wild, it is not all that helpful.

After leaving an abusive marriage, I depended on my logic to help me through the emotional roller coaster ride that I was on. My logic protected me and also prevented me from emotional meltdown. It was my survival guide.

I depended on my logic to help me deal with my separation from my marriage, and the loss of my father and dealing with health issues, which happened all around the same time. Like the saying goes, "when it rains, it pours." That's exactly how it felt. I could not allow any emotions to bury me alive, so my logic came to the rescue.

However, depending on my logic came with a price, which I did not realize for some time till I became aware of the fact that I was becoming a person lacking emotions. I felt that I was observing myself from the outside. I noticed that I had started to build a wall around my emotions, and that if I was not careful, I would lose this part of me, which I did not want to lose. Yet I was satisfied being a very logical person, and that made me a strong person.

Once I realized what was happening within myself, and how I was transforming into an emotionless person, I knew that I could not and should not let that happen; if I did, I would lose who I really am. So who was I really? I knew that I did not want to be a cold person.

I wanted to be a person that feels complete, meaning that I wanted to be a person that possesses both logic and emotion to have proper balance. I wanted to be a person that has compassion for others; yet at the same time, I wanted to be logical enough to not let emotion dictate my life. That could destroy me by making wrong decisions based on emotions. I also did not want logic to dictate me to become a cold, heartless person either.

Obstacle #1: Fear

What is fear? Fear is an emotion, aroused by an impending threat, danger, etc., whether real or imagined; however, the feeling of being afraid is real. It is very common for most people to experience fear in life. It is one of the most common and biggest obstacles in life. I don't care who says that they are fearless or do not fear anything at all. There is always a small area in which a person will, at one time or another, experience fear.

As a child, I feel I was pretty fearless in many areas of my life. I was not afraid of any challenges that a child would encounter. However, somewhere deep within me, there was some fear that I was not aware of. People who know me would not or could not imagine that I could possibly have any fears. They could not imagine it to be true, because of how I have overcome life's challenges.

This is when I can say that I had the courage to overcome fear, and I faced the challenges that life threw at me. I did go through all the fears that many people go through, when I first started to clear my path to a new life, a life of my own. The most common fear that most people will experience is not having the courage to overcome it—like the fear of what people will think; the fear of not doing what is right; the fear of not doing what is in alignment with their faith.

Generally, the fear of the outcome is also very common. I feared whether I would be able to manage to clear a path for me to move ahead; I feared making a mistake; I feared how my actions would affect anyone in my life. Fear was definitely present in my life. This is where logic and common sense was a big tool, like a hammer and chisel that helped me chip away at the big boulder that was blocking my passage.

It was not an easy task, but through hard work and determination, I chiseled away, because I had the vision of what lay ahead of me if I continued and not gave up. I needed the vision first, which motivated me to carry on, and that was why I hung onto the vision and feeling that I had experienced when I saw the movie, *Sleeping With the Enemy*—the feeling of joy of experiencing relief and freedom.

Fear has a tendency to keep popping up in life due to life circumstances that cause us blockages. It is up to us to find the courage to chisel it away. Realistically, fear is one obstacle that will continue to occur throughout our lives. I know this because I feel that even though I have overcome one obstacle, there are always new ones that will show up as I journey through life.

My initial obstacle was the fear of leaving my marriage. It is not really a Catholic thing to do, because I had taken a vow of "till death do us part." I felt that I was doing something wrong in the eyes of God. My other fear was that of being of Asian culture. It was about how my family or other people were going to react to my decision to leave my abusive marriage.

I was asked by a Baptist minister about why I was having difficulty making a definite decision to leave the abusive situation I was in. Was it because of being Catholic, or because of being Asian? I said it was both, and the next question was, what comes first—being Catholic or being Asian? Then the question was, what do you really want? My answer to that was that I just wanted to be on my own. I wanted to be alone. The next day, he showed up with a bible, and he showed me a quote that said that God does not intend for us to suffer.

Feeling the assurance that God does not intend for us to suffer, I felt comfortable to proceed with my decision to leave my marriage, and I was prepared to face whatever obstacles I may encounter along the way.

How Fear Has Taken Over

I could now start my journey to having a life. I hoped to start my own life, but even though I was able to overcome my fear that was blocking my route, I still had many more blockages to clear. What really helped me with clearing my blockage that I encountered was that I remained focused on my journey and did not let any distractions get in the way. I maintained control of my life and did not pay any attention to people that were not in line with my plan.

Fear has a tendency to creep up along my journey. After having chiseled away the big boulder of fear, and now that I was starting my journey as a single woman, bam! A big boulder fell upon my path in my new journey.

Now in my late 20s, I was faced with health issues. I was experiencing severe and constant pain.

Now my new journey began with finding out what the reason was for experiencing so much pain that I could barely stand or hold my breath. Tests after tests, and doctors after doctors, I was being told that I was experiencing psychosomatic pain. I was told that the pain was real but that it was psychosomatic, and it was brushed off. I have a high tolerance for pain, but I was not satisfied with being brushed off.

A few years passed, and I was still in search of answers. Finally, in my early 30s, with lack of treatment, I had now developed a tumor on my left ovary, which finally showed up on my ultrasound test.

That was when the doctor finally took me seriously and sent me for more tests. As time passed, the tumor not only grew but another one developed in my right ovary. While waiting for results and going for tests, I had multiple visits to emergency, with excruciating pain.

I was then finally scheduled for surgery to have the tumors removed. It was then that the doctors realized I had stage 4 endometriosis, and all my bowels were already affected by the disease.

After my surgery (my 2nd), the doctor informed me of my diagnosis. Unfortunately, there is no cure; however, there are treatments available, and it is very expensive—$400-plus a month.

This is when a new fear crept up. I was happy to have a name for the issues I was dealing with. It was no longer psychosomatic, but I was now bombarded with multiple thoughts in my head. My head was racing with so many thoughts that I could barely remember them all, except the most crucial ones.

I was now faced with new fears (my huge boulders). How was I going to work when I was in constant pain? It was similar to having labor pain. I know I have worked through my pain, but my fear was that there would be days when I would not be able to tolerate it, and I would end up in an emergency room, which by now was a monthly visit.

My hourly wage was low, and I was a freelance designer, which meant I did not have a regular weekly income. My fear now was how I would be able to manage to afford my treatments. Would I be able to work the hours I needed in order to help pay my regular monthly expenses plus my new expenses for my treatments. Plus, now that I was going to be recovering from surgery, I had no income—I don't get paid if I don't work. I felt my world come crashing down.

I was now faced with a situation where I could see all the boulders in front of me. I knew that in order for me to go forward, I would need to make sure that I was able to somehow break down this huge boulder in front of me. I needed to determine what tools I would need to help me break down this boulder. What tools would be the best? Did I have the tools? If not, what do I do?

Overcoming Fear

Fear is definitely the biggest obstacle I had. But like everyone else, I was not immune to this obstacle. In order for me to overcome this fear related to my health conditions, and move forward with all these challenges ahead of me, I made the decision that I was going to take control of the disease instead of the disease taking control of my life.

Making the decision to take control of the disease before it took control of me, helped me to charge forward and face whatever challenges I may encounter. I stopped the fear from taking over how I was to proceed further. I just concentrated on chipping away a bit of the boulder at a time, till I was able to clear a path to get further along in my journey.

Many of you probably experience fear as a stumbling block in many areas of your life, which probably stops you from taking action to move forward or even take chances in life. Many of you even allow the fear to take control of your life, because of the fear of the unknown.

Since most of you are not able to see what is beyond this big boulder, you wonder to yourself if it is worth it to move this boulder out of the way to find out what's ahead. At times, you may even ask yourself what would happen if you worked at removing this boulder, only to find out that maybe you really did not want to be on this path after all, and then find that you have wasted your time in chipping away at this boulder.

Sometimes you may wonder what would happen if you did chip away this boulder, only to find that beyond this boulder, there was yet another one for you to work at. With all these thoughts going through your head, it only makes you feel discouraged to actually take any action to overcome fear, and then you allow it to freeze you.

Like you, I too have had many thoughts take over my mind, but what I did was to make sure that I did not let all these voices take over my head and disrupt my intention of seeking my path that would lead me to take charge of my life.

I therefore had not given myself any choice to allow any interruption to creep in and take over to disrupt my journey.

It was important for me, to get me to where I wanted to be, so I needed to be focused on working on myself. I needed to make sure that I acquired skills and knowledge along the way, with experiences that would teach me to be strong and confident, to be able to face all the challenges that I would be faced with.

Some challenges were easier to deal with, and some were not. It all depended on the situation. Some were easier to deal with because I had learnt from experience how to deal with something that was similar but had different twists.

With some challenges, I needed to learn new skills to overcome them. As I proceeded in my journey to reclaim my life, I was acquiring numerous skills from experiences, so I would know how to reclaim my life. It was therefore important that I allow myself to take in all the lessons that I could learn along the way.

It was important that I pay attention and stay focused on my goals, and not let any obstacles discourage me from moving forward. It was very important for me not to give up. I needed to be a good example for my son, in that no matter what challenges life threw at me, I would not let it knock me down.

Obstacle #2: Courage

Courage is the ability to face challenges and difficulties without fear, or rather the quality of mind and spirit to face danger, pain, difficulties, etc., without fear, or in other words, to be brave. You and I both know that no one in this world is immune to life's challenges. It is how we handle the challenges that will determine if we are brave enough to face them.

Sometimes we really do not know how much courage we have within us until we are faced with difficulties, and with mental, emotional, and physical pain. We are faced with challenges in our work lives and home lives, and when we are faced with such challenges, it is up to us to decide whether we want to allow ourselves to live with the challenges that can rob us of our health and happiness, or whether we wish to change our circumstances.

For me, I made the decision for myself that I was not going to allow anyone, or any challenges, be it financial or health challenges, to pull me down. Therefore, I needed to overcome any fear I may have that would handicap me from moving forward or from growing.

By doing so, and being focused on my personal growth and knowing for myself what strength I have within myself to deal with life challenges, I was able to have the courage to tackle what lay ahead of me. My family has always said that I am stubborn, but I call myself determined, which is the very same trait but in a positive light. It's this very same trait that has helped me through all my challenges.

It was my determination that gave me the courage to carry on, and I still continue to carry on. Determination is what gives me the courage to continue to learn and grow every day. I know I will never stop learning, and I will never stop letting life educate me daily, and I know it will continue to do so till the day I die.

I would like to encourage you to be brave and believe in yourself that you are capable of overcoming anything life throws at you, if you allow yourself to overcome the fears that may handicap you. Sometimes we don't know that we are strong and that we have the courage to overcome anything. We won't know unless we are actually faced with difficulties.

It is up to us to decide whether we want to just give up because we feel we cannot overcome our fears, or whether we want to find out for ourselves if we are capable of overcoming them. Only then will we know for sure that we have some strength hidden inside, which we need to bring to the surface.

I did not have many resources or support available to me in my journey; however, I know that in this day and age, there are many resources that have become available to help people that are going through many life challenges.

I encourage you to please take advantage of the resources available, to help you in your journey to becoming a whole, strong, and confident person. Give yourself this gift of becoming who you are, and give yourself the opportunity to bring out your potential to be the person you want to be. Give yourself a chance to be happy being who you are and who you want to be.

If I can remotely make a minute difference in anyone's life, by sharing my story to help anyone in their life's journey, I will be happy to have taken this opportunity to make myself vulnerable and share my personal story.

Obstacle #3: Circumstances

In life, we often encounter unavoidable circumstances, which can be a very big blockage for us to move forward, without additional help outside of ourselves. It's like a huge boulder that is extremely hard for us to chip away with the tools we have.

In such a case, we will need to get additional help to move it away, like getting someone who can operate a bulldozer to lift it away.

Overcoming Obstacles

For me, my big boulder and unavoidable circumstance was dealing with health issues— my own as well as my father's.

My father was diagnosed with pancreatic cancer, and I was dealing with multiple health issues. At the time, it was mainly with the issue of dealing with a breast lump, which had been growing rapidly over a period of two years and had been ignored by the doctor, as they considered that being in my 20s was too young for them to be concerned.

However, dealing with these issues shortly after my exit from my marriage, I barely had time to even consider where I was going with my life. Since my family hadn't been in the country very long, I took the responsibility of taking my father for his weekly chemotherapy, since I was the only one with a vehicle.

I considered this as an obstacle or a storm, because it meant that I had to put everything on hold till this storm passed. While I was taking my father for his therapy, I was also dealing with my own doctors and the option to have surgery, and if need be, if the cancer had spread past the tumor, then I was to have radiation following the surgery. Luckily for me, I did not have to go through radiation, since removal of the lump was sufficient. This storm lasted about a year or so; therefore, my life of recovery from my separation from my marriage was on hold.

With such kinds of unavoidable circumstances, I was at the mercy of time. I could not predict how much time I would need in order to move forward to work on my life. In order to paint a picture in oil, it is important to prime the canvas—you cannot start without it. The unavoidable circumstance here was like priming a canvas first, to get the canvas ready in order to start painting. I needed time for it to dry before I could start to paint.

In some ways, life is like painting in oils: It takes time and patience to plan out the picture, time to mix colors, to paint a layer, and time to dry to get to the next step, layer after layer, before it can come together. The different layers represent different situations, experiences, and so on and so forth.

After having buried my father, I went in for my surgery the same week. In the meantime, I had been doing research for job opportunities in Vancouver, B.C., so that I could move there and start a new life, and give myself an opportunity to be away from all of the negativity around me in Toronto.

I needed to be away from everything and everyone, where there were too many unhealthy memories to remind me of daily. It felt as though the old pictures had too many dark colors painted over and over them, and that it would be difficult to have a fresh, new picture painted over it. I needed a fresh, new canvas and fresh new paints in order to start over. Going to B.C. was like my new canvas—a new city in a new province.

I started my journey to my new life, a life that was supposed to be mine. I thought that I did in fact now own my life, but little did I know that I really did not have it yet. I felt like I was free at the time, because I had left a life of imprisonment.

But in reality, I was not really all that free, because now I was a prisoner of my economics—but that was still better than the life that I previously had.

Obstacle #4: Financial Issues

Financial issues were definitely one of the unavoidable circumstances that caused delays. I left my marriage empty handed; I did not fight for my share of marital assets. I just wanted my peace of mind. The man I was married to, had too much greed, and he would give me eternal grief for money, so I saw no point in making the lawyers rich. We would also end up depleting any resources for my son's future.

People could not understand my decision to not fight for my share. For me, it was important to put my life back together sooner, and it was more worth it than spending years in grief from being in a legal battle. I had faith in myself to have the capability to rebuild financially. I felt it was far easier to do so with peace of mind than to be in a legal battle.

When I first left, I was literally penniless. I had acquired two additional employment positions, aside from my full time employment. Plus, I used my crafty skills and made crafts to sell, in order to help furnish my empty apartment. I was starting fresh, with absolutely nothing at all. I did not seek government assistance. I was not qualified for assistance because my rent was too high.

Even though I was not qualified for any assistance, I had no qualms of my own ability to support myself, as I knew in my heart that I possessed enough skills to find a way to do so. To me, financial burden was just one of the many stumbling blocks that was better than being caged in a blocked cell. I knew that in time I could overcome this stumbling block and get on my feet again.

I continued to stay focused on my journey of putting my life together. I did not and could not afford to allow any obstacles to get in the way of my journey. Although I was not fully clear of my destination as of yet, I was certain that I did not wish to be where I was. I knew that I needed to set goals for myself of what I would like to do with my future, but I was not able to do so without first removing all issues that kept popping up to put a stumbling block in my path.

I know for a fact that many people fear taking actions to help themselves out of an abusive or unhealthy relationship, due to financial situations, because they fear they will not be able to support themselves. Fear of being out on the streets, and fear of lack of finances, keeps them from taking the steps to free themselves from an unhealthy or abusive relationship, even at the risk of their own lives.

For me, I made the decision that my peace of mind and my sanity was more important than my economical comfort. Having that mindset, I did not fear that I would not be able to survive on my own.

I had faith and trust in my own skills and work ethics; and being a hard worker, I believed in myself, and that I would be able to put my life back in order. It was important for me to reach my goal with full determination. By being determined, it did not allow the fear of being poor to stop me from moving forward toward my goal of being my own person, and of living the life I wished to build for myself.

I think we must not be afraid of hard work. If we are willing to work hard for what we believe in, and are willing to work hard at earning a living, we will be able to survive no matter what hardships we may encounter.

Chapter 5

Steps to a New Life

New Beginning

In order for me to have a new beginning, it was important for me to go through the different phases of overcoming different blockages that I was to encounter: fear of the unknown, learning to overcome those fears, learning about my own abilities and strengths, and being aware of my own survival skills and how to implement them into my life so that I could move forward.

I was determined to carry on and not be discouraged by my financial situation. Many people fear leaving an abusive marriage or relationship for the reason of being unable to support themselves. They fear that they will not be able to manage.

For them to be comfortable financially is far better than being penniless, and so they remain in an unhealthy or abusive relationship far much longer than they should; or even in some cases, people never have the courage to leave. They decide that being abused or being in an unhealthy relationship is better than not having a comfortable materialistic lifestyle.

In order to have a new beginning, it was important for me to choose what was right for me. In my heart and mind, what was right for myself was my peace of mind. I wanted to be happy being the person I am from my core. In order for that to happen, I could not be in a relationship where my life was controlled by someone else.

51

I chose not to complain about my life, so I made the decision to do something about it so that I could be happy that I made my own choices, instead of them being made for me.

New Path

As I managed to chip away many of my blockages and the stumbling block that had barricaded me and imprisoned me for many years, I was finally able to get to the other side, to a new beginning and to a new world ahead of me.

When I got to the other side, the world ahead of me opened up, and what was ahead of me was so vast and open. There were many paths to take. Even though it was open and free and vast, it certainly did not mean that each path ahead was a smooth one. They all had their ups and downs, and some stumbling blocks here and there, but after having gone through the major hurdles, the blocks ahead did not seem all that difficult to push aside.

There were so many paths to choose from, and each path had its own unique trail. I have always been curious about all the different destinations, and I was always open to learning from life. Each path had valuable gifts awaiting, and I yearned for personal growth; therefore, I was willing to go on different paths in order to pick up various gifts of knowledge along the way.

I chose to be educated in many fields so that I would be skillful in many professions. Therefore, I would always have options to remain employed and not have to have financial worries, and thus not have to chisel a big blockage, as I am prepared with enough tools to be able to eliminate that blockage, should one arise.

One of the paths that I really wanted to be on ever since I was a teenager is the spiritual path. I have always wanted to be of service to mankind. I have always felt that my life was meant for something good. I wanted to make a difference and to be a difference. How I was going to do that, I did not know then. I will talk more about my spiritual journey in my next book.

New Skills

One of my passions in life is to continue to learn and grow. I have always been interested in learning new skills, especially where I can have my creative juices flowing. Although I majored in business and accounting in college, due to a lack of choices for education in creative arts, my passion for the creative arts remained alive in me, and I always dabbled in crafty projects.

I am a floral designer by profession. Due to health reasons, and because of the nature of the business that I freelanced as a designer, my job was very seasonal; hence, there were slow periods where there was no work available. In order to keep a steady stream of income, it was necessary for me to have a backup to supplement my income.

Being the responsible person that I was, I wanted to ensure that I was able to pay my monthly expenses in a timely manner and not be indebted to anyone. All through these periods, I had gone through 8 surgeries, two of which were major surgeries, and one of which kept me hospitalized for two and half months.

I made monthly emergency visits to the hospitals on a monthly basis for 7 years, and sometimes it would be an overnight stay, or a couple of days, or a week's stay, including being in the cancer ward for kidney obstruction.

While I lived through these health struggles, I continued on with my journey, and I was told by a specialist that because of the condition I had, I would die slowly and painfully. I did live with chronic pain and was heavily medicated to keep me alive and somewhat functioning.

Out of sheer determination, I did not allow my health conditions to stop me from continuing to get myself educated and to acquire new skills.

Over the years, I went back to school and took courses to get a diploma in special effects makeup. I also got certifications in Reiki, Reflexology, and teaching English as a second language. I took crystal healing, Past Life Regression Therapy, and various other workshops. I have put all of this education to good use in order to supplement my income.

I have always had a hunger and thirst for knowledge. To be able to learn, to me, is like being able to breathe and to be alive. I do not know what it would be like for me if I were to ever stop learning. I am more willing to pay to educate myself, more than I would be willing to pay for entertainment.

Learning and challenging myself is my life. I thrive on challenges. I thrive on achieving my goals in spite of my health challenges. I am always open to acquiring new skills and being educated in anything that sparks my interest. What can I say? I do have one curious mind that always needs to know the what, when, and why.

I feel like my brain needs to be constantly fed, and the hunger is too great to ignore. I am continuously searching for ways to curb hunger. I know that what I crave most of the time is knowledge related to life and people. I like to learn about people from different cultures and from different parts of the world, which peaks my interest in learning different languages so that I can communicate even briefly by greeting them in their language.

I speak about 7 languages and am fluent in 3. I can manage to make light conversation in the rest, and I can greet in more than 7 languages. I feel that the ability to be able to speak even a few words in other languages helps me to break the ice when meeting with people. It helps me to learn more, and it gives me the opportunity to learn more about people. I would love to acquire the skills to speak more languages should I have the opportunity. My desire to learn new skills will always be something to strive for.

Setting Goals

Setting goals was one key factor to help me attain my life of freedom. In fact, all of my life, that is exactly what I did. I planned and set goals for myself. Setting goals and achieving them was one of the main reasons that I managed to overcome many obstacles that came my way, including the unavoidable ones. My focus of achieving my goals was what kept me going, no matter what.

I feel that it is very important for everyone to have goals. Having goals in life is what makes life interesting; plus, it also helps a person to challenge themselves to see what their strengths and weaknesses are, and thus helps a person to know what they can do or are capable of doing for themselves, so that they can plan their lives according to their skills.

I know that for me, setting goals was important, and it did help me to be more aware of what my strengths and weaknesses are, or were. It also helped me to use my mental skills to work out my weaknesses, if any, to achieve them. Goals have the capacity to challenge me mentally and emotionally, as well as physically. When I found an area where I may have a weakness, I found a compromise in order for me to reach my goals, without compromising my goals. It was therefore important to have the mental capacity to be able to do so.

I must say that I was fortunate to have the mental capacity to handle many challenges that I faced throughout my life. It helped to lift me up when I was knocked down so many times. It helped me to remain sane through the darkest days of my life. But in all honesty, I believe that it was my guardian angels that helped me by giving me the gift of survival through my mind.

Having goals is what kept me going because it helped me to move forward to my journey in setting myself free from a life that I was trapped in. I believe that I survived my health challenges because I was so focused on reaching the goals that I had set for myself that it helped me forget my health issues. Because I was determined to reach my goals, I was able to set aside or endure my chronic pain that I was living with. I wanted so much to know for myself whether I was capable of achieving my goals, and to feel proud of myself that I did it.

In order to achieve anything we want in life, it is important for us to set a goal for ourselves, no matter how big or how small. Having goals gave me a purpose to live. My goal to be a good mother also gave me the purpose to make sure I survived my illness and was able to be around for my son.

I am not sure how life would be for me if I did not have a goal or have a purpose in life. To have no meaning to my life, it would not be a life. I always believe that my very existence has a purpose; therefore, I had to try my best to find out what my purpose was, and set a goal and achieve it.

Currently, my purpose in life is to make a difference in this world, and to have the ability to touch lives and help make a positive impact in someone's life. I want to bring healing to people's lives, and that is why I acquired the skills and knowledge to heal, so that I can fulfill the goal I have set for myself to be able to heal others. I worked on healing myself, and have succeeded in pulling myself from all the health conditions I lived with. I got myself off the medications that I had been prescribed for so many years. I am in better health now, and I hope to help others have better health as well.

Accomplishments

Having a determined personality, it is natural for me to be a person that sets goals for myself, and to be sure that I do indeed accomplish them as well. I thrive on accomplishments. From a very young age, I have always been somewhat competitive. Therefore, I would work very hard to make sure I succeeded in everything I did.

I participated in every competition the school organized when I was in school. From sports, speech, art, to fashion shows—you name it— I participated. I was always in the top three; I have won in every competition I participated in. That is what I call accomplishments.

This very attribute of mine was indeed very prominent in all aspects of my life. I always made sure that I did my best in everything that I set out to do, both professionally and personally. I always put my heart and soul into what I did, and once I set my mind to something, I would work towards accomplishing it.

I was always told that I was my own worst enemy because I had very high expectations of myself, which I did indeed. I was competitive, more for myself, and I had this need to know what I was capable of. The competitive nature was not about being competitive with others, but rather within myself about my own capabilities and possibilities.

My mind was in constant overdrive, on problem solving, how to deal with issues that may arise, and what the solutions were to a problem. I always believe that there are solutions to a problem; hence, I strive to seek solutions to every problem, and work to achieve them. Achievement means accomplishment.

Accomplishing goals is very important to me, and I have managed to do so in many areas of my life. As mentioned earlier, since I managed to heal myself to better health, my current goal now is to help others to achieve better health, whether it be physical health or mental health. I think this is now my lifelong goal, and I can proudly say that I did successfully achieve these goals with people I worked with or worked on.

My hope is to continue on this journey to bring healing to all those in need, and to continue to be successful in achieving this goal for the rest of my life. I feel that I did indeed find who I am and what my purpose in life is, and that I am living that purpose.

Although at this time in my life, this is what my purpose is, I am still open to what life may bring to me in the future. I am ready for any new calling or new purpose that life may present to me, and I will be happy to set the goal and achieve it. I will never give up on growing and improving myself.

I believe we all must always be open to embrace what life has to offer us, and to accept all it has to offer, good or bad, with grace and gratitude.

When we have gratitude in our hearts, we are bound to achieve all that we wish for. With the attitude of gratitude, we are able to attract positivity into our lives.

Satisfaction

Satisfaction is a state of fulfilment and contentment.

It was important for me to be content or feel contentment in life, so it was necessary for me to go through all the above steps of setting goals and working towards achieving them. I did not only want to achieve my goals, but I wanted to achieve them with excellence, and that is why I put my heart and soul into the task at hand.

Achieving my goals with excellence is what brought me great satisfaction. That is when I feel content with my efforts that I put into the things I do in life. In doing so, I can feel a certain pride within that I left no stone unturned.

Life itself is complicated, so it isn't always so easy for many to determine their life's mission and goals. Challenges and distractions crop up along the way, which can easily deter a person from staying focused on their own life, or what they want to do or where they want their life to be by a certain age.

People get so busy dealing with the challenges that show up, and then the distraction shows up. While dealing with the challenges, they feel so overwhelmed by it that they feel the need to put their life's dreams and goals on the back burner, and before you know it, years fly by, and people continue to deal with all the challenges and distractions.

As for myself, I never wanted to put anything on the back burner...I was all about making sure that nothing or no one knocked me down in any way, shape, or form. However, there were times that I did have to put some things on the back burner due to unavoidable circumstances, such as emergency health situations that needed to be addressed before everything else, but my goals were never forgotten. They just remained on hold, ready to be executed as soon as I could manage and proceed to reach for my goals. For me, my biggest challenge was my severe, multiple health conditions, which could easily have kept me bedridden; however, I made the decision that I was not going to let my health issues take over my life, or have control over me. I made the decision that it was me who was going to be in control of my life, and not my health challenges.

It was not very easy, as I lived with chronic and debilitating pain daily, and I needed 3 hours upon waking to prepare myself to start my day, in order to have the ability to be functional. I lived my life as if I was worry free and pain free. People weren't really aware of the fact of what I was living through.

People just viewed me as someone who was goal oriented and determined to achieve all I set out to achieve. I had not made it known to others what daily struggles I lived with, or how much willpower I needed to present myself as someone that is healthy and full of life. The days when it was extra rough, I felt it would be obvious for others to see that I was not well.

I would slap on some makeup to hide the pain that was showing on my face, and I put every ounce of energy into appearing and sounding healthy and well. It gave me great satisfaction to know that I had the strength and determination and ability to hide my health struggles daily, and that I tried to live a life that others would imagine as problem free.

When I think of how I was able to do that, it made me aware of my strength, courage, and determination, and all these traits that I possessed made me feel proud of myself and gave me great satisfaction.

Chapter 6

Learning About Myself

Awareness

Awareness is one of the key ingredients that we need in order to have a better understanding of ourselves. There is a saying: "We learn something new every day." It is true that we do.

I find I am always learning something new about myself. I feel that with every new day, comes new experiences. Some days I may have an idea of what to expect of my day, but most days I never know what is ahead of me.

It is the unexpected event that takes place and how I face it that helps me be more aware of myself. It is how I face the situations that tells me more about myself, because at the end of the day, I have a tendency to go over in my head of how I handled my day. I analyze the situations and my actions, and I get a feel for how much of my actions resonated with me. This gives me a new awareness of me as a person.

I think there were times when I may have dismissed some of the new awareness I may have for myself, perhaps because I was not ready to embrace it. Or perhaps I may have made excuses to dismiss it due to the fear that I may not have been ready to embrace my awareness.

I think there was a part of me that was not ready to embrace my true self, because a part of me was not ready to face what lay ahead of me if I were to truly be myself—how would people accept the change in me?

There were times when I did not want to admit that I had a weakness, and that would prevent me from being truly aware of who I am. I guess I did not want to admit that I had a weakness somewhere, because I was overall a strong person, and most people did see that, and I did not want to admit and face the weakness that I had.

You are now probably wondering what weakness I could possibly be talking about. After all, up until now, from what you have read, you may have gathered that everything I have dealt with did in fact take a lot of courage, and that I must be a strong person.

It is true that I had to be strong to have gone through all that, yet here I was, still learning about myself. That is the reason I say I became aware of some weakness I had, and you are probably wondering what it could possibly be.

For years, I worked at a job being overworked and underpaid, and I did nothing about it. I am very good at what I do, and I am a very efficient worker. My weakness here was that I did not give myself value, and I did not value myself enough to charge the rate that I was worth, and rightfully for the services I provided. I gave myself the excuse that I did not do that because I was grateful for the job I had, and that I should be grateful.

There were also times when I did not speak my mind because I felt I did not want to be rude and did not want to hurt people's feelings. I knew I was blunt and was told that I shoot from the hip, yet I began to realize that there were some circumstances in which I didn't know why, so I had to examine the situation and ask myself why I didn't. I then realized that I just didn't want to be confrontational with some people who were narcissistic.

This new awareness motivated me to make the necessary changes I needed for my personal growth. I made sure that people valued my worth as I did, in my profession. I spoke my truth as I wished, no matter what circumstance. I felt that as long as I spoke my truth and did not offend anyone, there was no reason for me not to. If they took offence, then it was something they needed to look at in themselves.

I feel that no matter how old we get, we never stop learning about ourselves; therefore, I am not surprised with each passing year that I learn something new about myself. By being aware, we can grow and change to become a better person.

I always suggest that people pay attention to every detail about themselves. Our reactions to our situations will give us clues about ourselves. When we are able to observe ourselves well, then we will be able to grow and change to be a better person. We then make conscious efforts to grow and improve.

Acceptance

I am pretty sure that everyone goes through the thought of acceptance. Many people go through their entire life seeking acceptance. Fear of not being accepted, from childhood, makes people lose themselves. For some, they even join the wrong crowds just to feel that they belong.

To some people, a sense of belonging is so great that it can sometimes make them lose their good judgement. Especially if they are emotionally and mentally weak, they may fall prey to some cult members or leaders who end up brainwashing these vulnerable people.

For me, I feel fortunate that the faith I had within me helped me accept myself for who I am or was all my life. I was termed as different due to my spiritual gifts, and I always felt different and like an outsider. I could not relate to most people that I knew. Growing up, I was not quite aware about these spiritual gifts; I always shrugged the experiences off as being my imagination.

Having a creative flair, and interests in arts and crafts, it was natural for me to be imaginative; hence, I shrugged my spiritual experiences off as my wild imagination. Fortunately, I accepted my wild imagination, as part of me didn't think too much about it.

From a very young age, I did not care if anyone accepted me for who I was just because I was different. Having such an attitude did help me to be strong and face a lot of my life's challenges. I am sure that somewhere, at some time, I may have wished to be accepted by my peers. The only time I can remember when I felt somewhat out of place was during my school years.

Having skipped a few classes, I was always the youngest amongst my classmates, and during my teenage years, being 2 to 3 years younger than my classmates was a big difference. I could not relate to them in many ways. I was mature at a very young age, and I felt more mature than my classmates, even though they were two to three years older than me.
I think being comfortable with who I was, and accepting myself for who I was, helped me to endure every roadblock that I faced, which led me to overcome all obstacles to being my true self.

Being my true self is by no means an easy task or journey, but with persistence and having faith and belief in God and myself, I reached my goal and destination of being who I am today.

I have gone through quite a painful journey to get to where I am. I have been knocked down repeatedly, at different stages of my life, but fortunately, I did not remain down. I held my head high and continued.

After being knocked down repeatedly, I learnt how to keep my balance to prevent myself from falling all the way. Eventually, I learnt to duck and avoid being knocked down.

It was these very lessons of how to not let others knock me down that taught me how I could be my true self and be able to stand tall and strong.

Conscience

Conscience is the ethical and moral principles that control or inhibit the actions or thoughts of an individual. I believe that before we can be our true selves, it is important for us to question our own sets of moral values. What do we truly believe in? How do we want to conduct ourselves in our lives? How do we want to be treated, and how do we treat others?

I often find myself assessing my own behaviors after every difficult interaction I have with anyone. You could say that I do like to examine my own actions, or sometimes when I am faced with a difficult situations, I like to examine and analyze the situations or predicaments I may be in, so I would be very careful in my actions or reactions, as I like to be sure that my actions are not hurtful to others.

I feel it is important for me to be compassionate towards others, and in order for me to be my authentic self or my true self, I like to be sure that I do have a clear conscience within me.

If I can be clear of conscience in my actions towards others, then I should feel proud of myself that I am who I am, or who I want to be in this life. For me, it was important to live my life with a clear conscience.

I think our conscience is our campus to our soul. It is what guides us to be as good a person as we want to be.

Transition

Transition is moving from one position to another, or to make changes. After having lived a life based on what everyone in my life wanted of me, from the time I was born, I can truly say that I was not really living a life that I had really wanted or designed for myself.

Living a life based entirely on what was expected of me did not exactly feel right to me. I think I would have preferred to have made my own choice of what I was willing to do to meet those expectations. Choosing to meet the expectations of others by choice is living a life by choice.

When I was young, I was not aware that I had a choice, because it was drummed into my head that I must do as I am told. It is understandable that when I was young, it was necessary for me to do as I was instructed. After all, I was in an early stage of learning all about life.

As I grew older, having gone through life experiences, it taught me more about myself. I started to become more aware of what my personal preferences were. I have learnt to understand more of what resonates with me and what does not.

I also learnt what kind of people I prefer to keep company with, and who to avoid.

What I learnt the most in life for myself was that I valued family and friends more than material gains. I also learnt that it is the people in my life that either drained me or energized me. I learnt to value people that resonated with me. It is the people that pass through my life that are the reasons for my personal growth, be it emotional, mental, or spiritual.

Being a very intuitive person, I am able to gauge my own feelings and senses regarding people and situations that surround me. Therefore, I easily determined what resonated with me, sooner than most people would. However, like many of you, we can also be fooled by people who do not show their authentic selves.

I learnt that even though I knew that I was living a life based on what was expected of me for years, I knew that it did not totally make me happy. I am by nature a positive person, and I always see the positive side to everything; therefore, I am considered to be a happy and cheerful person. I knew deep down that even though I was able to be positive most of the time, there was a part of me that was still trying to live in a way that kept people around me happy.

This carried on for years. I then started to delve deeper into my soul, and I asked myself why I was still feeling somewhat imprisoned. Why was I still living a life of what was expected of me by my family, friends, and peers? I told myself that I did not have anyone over my head dictating how I should or should not live. As that clarity came to me, I asked myself why I carried on as if I was being dictated how to live.

When I had more clarity about my life and how I was carrying on, I made the decision to make the transition to being my authentic self. Making the transition was not as easy as I thought. There was a lot of thought that went into self-acceptance, my own set of values, and how my actions in life would affect those around me. I asked myself if I could still be the kind and caring person that I expected myself to be, and if I would lose myself from this transition.

Being a deep thinker, I tend to analyze things to minute details. I needed to understand, for myself, in which area of my life it was that I was being my authentic self, and where I was still stuck in the mindset of what was expected of me. I asked myself how I could make the transition so that I could be happy with the decisions I made, and so that the actions that I took did not hurt others. I also did not want to feel like I was compromising myself.

Like any lifestyle habits, changes do not happen overnight. All in all, I was really living my life as I pleased. I have always been a strong person, mentally and emotionally. People often sought me for advice, so why did I still feel like I wasn't really living as my true self?

Action Towards Transition

If I was already living a life pretty much as how I wished to live, or as who I wished to be, then what do I mean by being my authentic self, as you may be wondering now? I think I felt like I was not really living as my true self because there were some areas of my life where I felt like I was still on autopilot, from a lifetime of programming how I was to behave with people around me.

Although I am known to be blunt and direct, or as I am told, to shoot from the hip, there was still a side to me that was careful with my words or how I communicated. Therefore, in some communication with others, I still held my tongue for what I considered to be out of respect or out of being sensitive to people's feelings.

Then there were some areas in my professional life where I felt I did not value myself enough. I worked extremely hard, and I was very dedicated, loyal, and reliable. I allowed the employers to get away without showing my true worth to the company.

I was patient and put up with nonsense that did not serve my highest good. Perhaps somewhere deep inside, I felt that I needed to do this to remain employed. From the outside, I was viewed as someone who spoke up and always stood up to my employers.

I would quit but would always go back after being called to return. Come to think of it, I would say that it almost sounds like a bad relationship that is on again and off again. The only comforting thought to this is that the employer saw the value of my work and skills, enough to want me to return after quitting. I never asked for a raise, because I felt that the request may not be met. So for fear of disappointment, I never broached the subject, and I carried on working for rates that were far lower than my worth. When I became more aware that I did not value myself as I should in every way, I felt the need to take action to make the transition to my true self.

Taking Action

For many years, I felt like I was really living a life of my own. I thought I was because I was aware that I was a strong person, and I generally spoke my mind. It was not really easy for many people to walk all over me, because I did not let anyone walk all over me—I made sure of that after leaving my abusive marriage.

I was happy that I was finally living my own life. People respected me for the strength I had, which was an obvious trait that I had, and I helped many people to also have strength and move on and away from stressful environments. I even helped people with different strategies to cope with the challenges they were facing.

I carried on as I did, being this strong woman who had overcome all of life's challenges. So why did I still feel as though I was not being my authentic self? I just had this nagging feeling that I still had a lot to learn about myself. With this nagging feeling, I started to pay attention to myself, my life, my interactions with others, how I felt with each situation I dealt with, and how my reactions were with each situation and why.

Having paid close attention to myself, I was able to come to the conclusions to the awareness I had mentioned above, about how I did not value myself enough professionally, and how I held my tongue because of thoughts of not hurting others.

When I first realized that, I knew I had to make the changes I needed in order to feel like my true self. The only way to do that was to make sure that I accept my true value, and accept the fact that I should respect myself enough to truly speak my mind when someone tries to minimize me and my value. Standing up to my value should be more important than worrying about the feelings of those who are disrespecting me indirectly.

That is when I finally made the full transition to what I feel today as being my true self. I am sure that as life progresses, I will for sure encounter new life experiences and challenges, and I know I will have to face it the way I know how or want to be.

Becoming self-aware was the first step I learnt in being my true self. After that is understanding who I want to be and what kind of person I want to be in this life. With careful analysis, I was able to conclude how I should approach various situations or people that felt right for me and my core being.

I am happy that I was able to finally recognize which steps I needed to take in order to be my true self. With that knowledge, I implemented it into actions. I took the necessary actions to be who I wished to be—my true self.

Just being aware of how we wish to live our lives is useless without taking the necessary steps or actions towards our goals. It is important for me to overcome all my fears of how people would view me if I lived a life that I wished to live, and if I had the courage to really be who I wished to be by taking the actions to be so.

Chapter 7

Why Be My True Self?

Realization

I ask myself: Why be my true self now? For the majority of my life, I never really thought about it, because I was busy living it, battling with life's challenges as they surfaced. Oftentimes, it really felt like I barely had any breaks between challenges, so the thought of being my true self definitely was nowhere near my headspace.

Since I had been so busy battling with life's challenges, the years spent with the struggles was a time that was more about growing and learning how to deal with them. This time of going through different situations in life was like being in primary school, getting our early education.

As we advance in years, we start to figure out what we want to do with our lives, and what careers we wish to enter into, and then we decide to choose what subjects we want to major in so that we can gear towards the profession we want to enter into. As we start to narrow down what subjects we want to take up as our major, it helps us figure out if it's the route we want to take for our future.

Life's circumstances are very similar to what helps lead us to what or who we wish to be. Life educates us to learn more about ourselves; it teaches us how to deal with the challenges, and teaches us about our own strengths and weaknesses that lead us to our own realization of who we want to be in this life.

Life's challenges taught me everything I needed to know about myself. It taught me how to overcome all difficulties, taught me compassion, taught me skills to navigate through life, how to use my own experiences to help others going through difficulties, and how to share what I have learnt in life to help others to be courageous enough to weather the storms.

For me, I feel that my realization of wanting to be my true self came about when I was at a point in my life where I had learnt that life had taught me how to face all challenges with ease and grace. At this stage of my life, I knew I was not going to let anyone or anything knock me down. I felt that I was able to pick myself up with ease when I was knocked down.

I was happy with myself for everything that I had accomplished with my personal growth. Life carried on, yet there was still something that nagged at me that I was still not quite where I wanted to be.

The circumstances involving the change I needed to make for myself were so subtle that they just did not stick out. It was not really a change of how to handle life challenges, but more of a personal change that I needed to make from within.

It took me time to really do lots of self reflecting on what or who it was that was bothering me, or what it was that was making me feel that I still needed to grow and change. What were the changes that I needed to make in order to be my true self, and ones that I could be happy with?

Deep reflection and paying close attention to my day to day events helped me to realize what it was that I needed to do in order to be my true self, as mentioned above. I think when I first came to my realizations of what I needed to do, it did not feel as easy to make the change or deal with it as easily as it did with many other life challenges.

Life's challenges somehow did not seem as difficult to overcome, because logic helped find solutions to deal with them. It was merely following the logic that helped deal with it, and I successfully overcame it.

The final steps that I needed to take in order to be my true self were a bit more complicated, because it was a change that needed to be made, which involved both logic and emotions to deal with it. For me, dealing with situations with logic was far easier than with emotions; therefore, that was why it took me time to really accept the need to make the changes.

Desire

To desire is to want, to wish or long for. When we want to reach a goal or make any changes in our lives, it is important to have the desire to do so. The desire is always a driving force for us to reach our goal.

I have always been like a sponge when it came to learning. My curiosity to learn everything that I could learn is what gave me the desire to learn. I always felt the desire and the longing of educating myself in everything that caught my interest.

Having a curious mind and the constant need to learn and grow gave me the desire to get myself educated in all of the things that I wanted to learn and do. My desire to learn did not limit things that I was interested in.

I had the desire to learn about things even though they were not my primary interest, but more for practical reasons. Sometimes I had the desire to learn things just because it was a challenge. For some reason, I always had the desire to challenge myself to see what I was capable of.

It was my desire to challenge myself that helped me with dealing with all of my life's issues. No matter what we do in life, in order for us to be successful, it is important for us to have the true desire to do what we set out to do. Desire is what will fuel our motivation to achieve our goals.

For me, learning and continuing to learn and educate myself is one of life's most essential needs, just as we need air to breathe. I am always open to learning and growing daily. Because of this need to learn, comes the desire—the desire to pursue my goals, to be a better person, to be of service to mankind.

Implementation

As mentioned above, it is important to take action in order to follow through, no matter what we decide to do in life. I have always done my best to implement any thoughts or ideas I have come up with. It is necessary to do so in order for me to see my goals to fruition.

I am by no means perfect. Like everyone else, I too go through my moments of weakness, and moments of procrastination. As much as people view me as someone who works extremely hard, I do have my lazy moments as well. I think I have lazy moments, perhaps because I have a tendency to have high expectations of myself.

I believe that because I have high expectations of myself, I always make sure that I always implement all plans and ideas to achieve all goals, no matter how big or small, or how difficult or easy. Just having the desire to make a change in life, or to achieve a goal, is not sufficient. Desire is the first step. It is necessary to implement the desire into action.

When the desire is strong, it does help to motivate us to implement our desire into action. However, sometimes we may still have a strong desire, and if we still do not implement our ideas into actions, we will not accomplish our goals. There are also other factors to take into consideration for us to really implement what we want to do.

I know for a fact that there are so many factors to consider, because I have spent a great deal of time in my head, analyzing and feeling everything before I took actions to implement the plan. I was told that I have a tendency to analyze everything to minute detail.

Aside from analyzing things, I also need to feel things out. Before making any decisions or taking any actions, I like to make sure that my mind and my heart meet somewhere in between. For me, it is important that my logic and emotions meet to avoid any regrets.

Logic

I think logic is a very important quality to have. I think and feel that logic has helped me survive the most traumatic times of my life. I depended on logic to help me cope. It helps to show a clearer view of the situation at hand. Logic is also helpful with solutions to problems.

I always used logic to help cope whenever I encountered painful challenges in my life, namely during my marriage breakdown. I somehow managed to shut off my emotion switch and operate purely on logic. It was very helpful because I needed it to plan out my life step by step as to what I needed to do to move forward.

I needed my logic to help me put my life back together. I could not afford to allow emotions to drag me down and destroy me, or keep me down. Logic was my saving grace at the time I needed it. As I slowly started to put my life in order, I realized that I had allowed logic to take over my life.

I found that somehow in the process of trying to survive, I was living mainly in my head. My life was all about solving one problem after another, and I felt that I could not afford to get emotional, which would break me down into pieces, and I wouldn't be able to think straight or function.

I made certain that I needed to keep all my emotions in check or even locked up. What I did not realize was that over time, I buried my emotional being so deep inside me, and soon logic took hold of my life. It was fine when I needed it to help me survive all the challenges.

Once I learnt all the skills of coping with life's issues, I felt that I did not need my logic as my crutch anymore. But since logic was in so much control of my life, I started to feel like I was no longer who I was or wanted to be.

Emotion

Emotion is the conscious state of feelings of joy, happiness, fear, and hate, or a psychological state or reaction to an event. All human beings are emotional beings, except for psychopaths, who lack the emotional connection to humans; they lack empathy or remorse.

In order for me to feel like a true human being or a decent person as a whole being, I need to be a person that has both the qualities of logic and emotion. When I went into my survival mode, and buried my emotions so deep inside me that I think I lost my emotions, it was like losing my humanity.

I noticed that I was always functioning from a place of logic, which to me seemed like losing a very important part of myself. Being logical, I was spared the feeling of emotional hurt and pain. I was spared the feeling of joy as well. That was when I realized I was missing a big part of myself that made me who I was—a part of me who I was proud of; a person that had compassion and love for others.

I was living in Vancouver when I went through this experience where I started to notice that I was lacking emotion. In spite of the fact that

I thought I had buried my emotions, I somehow knew within me that I did not like this new me, a person that didn't allow any emotion to surface. I did some soul searching and concluded that I did not want to be a cold, heartless, emotionless person. It simply is not who I wanted to be.

Having concluded that my logic was too strong and too much in control, I thought I would need help to bring out my emotional side so that I could be whole again. I contacted a counsellor at YWCA and requested an appointment to meet. The counsellor whom I met with wanted to know why I needed to meet with her.

I told her that I wanted to be whole again. I had buried my emotions so deep inside me that I was afraid that I would not be able to pull them out. I had become too logical, and being too logical was making me incomplete. I didn't want to be this cold, logical person that I was now. I became this logical person to survive my life, but I think it has gone too far.

She suggested that we play a game to determine how strong of a hold my logic had over my life. After playing this game, she determined that my logic would not give up control of my life. What she did not tell me at the time was that she felt she was not going to be able to help me bring out my emotions again, as my logic was too much in control.

We had decided that I would visit with her once a week to try to help me bring out my emotional side. However, before I could go back to my next appointment, I was sick with influenza. I took the day off from work as I was just too sick to get out of bed; if I could get out of bed, I would still go to work.

Since I was too sick to get myself to work, I was at home, sick and bored. I started to go through family photos, and there were voices in my head all the while—a whole debate was going on. It was a debate between my logic and my emotions; the logic being angry that I was too weak to drag myself off to work—blah blah blah.

My emotions were defending me, that I was just simply too sick to drag myself out, and that my body was too weak to work. As this debate carried on while I was going through family photos, I came across a photo of my parents, which was taken during the last few weeks of my father's life.

Upon seeing the photographs, I started to bawl, as I had just lost my father a few months earlier, and in my effort to stay strong for my family, I did not grieve as I should have. While I was bawling so hard, the voices in my head, between logic and emotions, were having a heated argument: "Stop crying," and, "No, I will cry all I want." Then suddenly, I felt myself rise above both my emotions and logic, and I made the decision that I would do as I pleased—no logic and no emotion was going to take control of my life—I decided to be in charge. I would be logical when I pleased, and I would be emotional when I pleased.

When this happened, I felt such a relief. I knew then and there that I was no longer controlled by my logic.

I, Jacinta, am now in control of *me*. I am whole again. I am no longer the cold, logical person that I had started to think I was becoming. I immediately called the counsellor to let her know that I no longer needed her help to find my emotions, but she insisted that she see me, and she wanted to know why I no longer needed to meet with her.

In my next meeting with her, I relayed my story about my heated arguments between my logic and emotions, and how I decided to take charge and shut them both up.

It was then that she said she was happy that I had managed to solve my own issues. When she met me at my first appointment the week prior, she felt she could not or would not be able to help me, because the signs of my logic wanting to be in control were too strong, and she had a hard time imagining if she would be able to help.

She said she never thought it was possible for me to be able to feel emotions again, and was at a loss and did not know how she could or would be able to help me with my request for help. She said she was truly happy that she didn't need to worry about it anymore.

She said she had never felt so helpless when she first saw me, and she felt that she had no knowledge of how to find a solution to my issue. She thought it would be a miracle for my logic to give up control.

Being Whole/Being Complete

After going through the battle between my logic and emotions, I was happy that I felt whole again. I had never realized in all the time that I was so busy learning to cope with life's challenges that I had allowed myself to be lost in the midst. I allowed my logic to take myself over. Who would have thought it was possible?

First, I battled to be free of being in control by my family life that I was raised in, and then it was setting myself free from being controlled by my married life. No one would really imagine that we sometimes need to set ourselves free from a part of our own self that is holding us back.

For me, it was the logic part that took control and made me devoid of emotions. I was fortunate that even though my logic had strong control over my life, my mental side was aware of the fact that my logic was taking hold of me, and that being too logical was not who I really wanted to be.

I am glad that as soon as I became aware of what I was dealing with within myself, I made sure that I did something to resolve the issues I was now facing within myself. I am also glad that I have a habit of doing self-reflection and soul searching, and I try to understand my purpose in life.

It is because of my need to be a better person that I tend to examine myself, my attitude towards life, how I treat others, and how I react to different people and circumstances. I think by having this nature about me in my subconscious mind, it led to my self- discovery of what my logic was doing to me.

My discovery led me to work on myself, to become whole and complete—a person with healthy logic and emotion—as we need both these traits to be complete.

Chapter 8

Discovering Myself

Self-Discovery

On a regular basis, on different occasions, I would often hear talk about self-discovery or finding oneself. In fact, there are workshops available for people to learn how to find themselves.

I was not aware of any of the above workshops that were available. I was too busy dealing with daily struggles, and learning how to survive from one challenge to the next. It is through all of my life experiences that led me to understand myself better.

Experiences, and how I dealt with them, made me become more self-aware.

Dealing with various people with challenging personalities, it was my habit to examine my own actions on how I handled my interactions with others, and that helped me to be aware of who I was and what kind of person I wanted to be.

I may think that I have discovered myself wholly; but truly, I really cannot say that for sure, because I am still on my journey in life. I may feel that I am really who I am and want to be, which may be true. I am my true self today from the experiences I have been through, and I know that my growth does not stop here.

I know that I am growing and evolving every day, from daily experience. For a long time now, I have felt that I have discovered myself, which I did; yet since I started to write this book, very recently, I have experienced something that opened up a whole new discovery of myself.

I feel that I have overcome all of my fears; I have emotional and mental strengths, and I am independent and self-sufficient. Yet a very recent experience helped me to become more aware of myself. I feel that this new experience made me more aware of the fact that there is still a part of me that needs to grow. I feel that there is a part of me that still has some fear that I have not yet overcome. The fear that I need to overcome is the fear of being vulnerable. I am sure that everyone lives through this fear, and I can almost guarantee that no one is immune to this.

Since I started to write this book I have written pretty much about everything that I have overcome to be my true self, and this new awareness of my fear of being vulnerable is pretty thought-provoking.

What I have come to realize is that I am always learning and growing every day. I am my true self now, as of now, from my life experiences I have accumulated over the years. I know for a fact that my learning and growing will never stop as long as I live.

Since I am aware of the fact that I wish to be an authentic person, I will always strive to learn and grow and be the best version of myself. I feel that there is a comfort in knowing that I try to be authentic, and that helps eliminate the stress of keeping up with appearances.

I take pride in the fact that I am always willing to better myself. I have never allowed any life challenges to cause me to be a bitter or angry person. It is a known fact that difficult situations in life can make us angry or bitter, or we can learn from the experience, and become a better person and use the experiences we encountered to help others. When we keep a positive attitude and allow love to flow within us, we are better able to tackle life's most difficult situations, and be a better person.

Why Self-Discovery?

Why do we need to discover ourselves? Is there a need? No, not really, if you like to just zip through life asleep—yes, asleep, and I don't mean literally asleep, but rather unaware. There are many people who do in fact go through life being unaware.

I would call people who were totally oblivious to all that goes on around them. I feel many go through life in this manner because they do not like to take responsibility for themselves. They have a tendency to blame everyone else for their problems, or for what goes wrong in their lives.

When people go through life in such a manner, they tend to lack the desire to grow and believe in self-improvement, and I think they also tend to be skeptical in many ways, in different areas of life. I think they tend to be skeptical all around. They would also lack faith; hence, when problems arise in life, they blame God for their problems if there is no one they can actually blame.

I do realize that everyone has their own path in life, their own life choices, their own beliefs, and their own opinion. I am merely stating my own thoughts and beliefs here, and my own opinion. It is really not meant to judge anyone for their journey.

I am expressing my thoughts and opinion based on my own life's journey to my self-discovery, and it is not meant to trigger anyone. I am sharing my journey as I feel that some of you may be able to resonate with my journey, and perhaps may be able to have a takeaway that may help you in yours.

Pre Self-Discovery

How was I before I started my journey to my self-discovery? At the time, I really just lived my life following the expectations of others.

Basically, I would say that I lived a life trying to fulfill the expectations of my parents, being an obedient daughter, as that was the norm for everyone; obey all the rules without questions, as the role of a child is to follow the rules that are laid out by the parents at home, and to follow the rules that are laid out by the teachers or the principal at school.

As I entered into adulthood, still very much controlled by my parents or family members, it was not exactly easy to have self-discovery. Once my marriage was arranged, the role of the person that controlled my life changed from my parents to my new husband and family.

Having lived a life that was pretty much controlled by others, I felt like I did not exist. The role I played was that of a person who just lived and existed, following the directions of people in my life.

Having a life that was not only being controlled by others but was also in an emotionally abusive environment, became too much for me. I started to feel that I needed to be my own person. I wanted to be free of everyone else's control. Making the decision to break free from that life, to go on a quest to search for myself, was not an easy decision, nor was the transition an easy one.

The need to break free from that life was so great that I felt that I simply had no other option but to finally make the decision to do so. There were also other mitigating factors that led to my making the ultimate decision to do so.

Once the decision was made, I moved forward and never turned back, and I never regretted the decision to do so.

During Self-Discovery

During the process of self-discovery, I couldn't really say that I was really aware of the journey I was on. I think I was merely on autopilot, just surviving through life's challenges that I was faced with. Facing challenge after challenge was what led me to be more aware of who I was from within, and who I wanted to be.

It was the process of realization of who I was and who I wanted to be that led me to muster up the courage to overcome fears and be the person I wanted to be. It was not an easy decision as there were many hurdles along the way. The main hurdles were to be confident enough not to care about what people would think of me or how people would judge me.

It was important for me to realize that I am the only one that truly knows what it feels like to be in my shoes, and that I need to be comfortable in them, as I am the one that will be walking in them my entire life. I also knew that people do have a tendency to judge and make assumptions. The fear of being judged, and the fear of not pleasing people, is one sure way of preventing my own personal growth and self-discovery.

Many people live a life based on what others think, or on the fear of being judged, which prevents them from being their authentic self. They in turn sacrifice what they truly want to do, and how they want to live their life, just because in their mind they fear not having the approval of their family.

Family can either be a great support in our lives or a great hindrance. I felt that if and when there was no support, it was up to me to decide for myself what was important for me. I needed to decide for myself if I had to go against all odds and work at becoming the person that I wanted to be, in order to be my true authentic self that I could be proud of.

Post Discovery

After years of facing challenges and learning and growing from the different challenges I faced in life, I can safely say that I have discovered myself and know who I am and what I am all about. I am aware of my calling in life. I am aware of the journey I am taking.

Through my life experiences, I have learnt to overcome many fears, and I have gained an enormous amount of knowledge to survive every challenge I am faced with. I learned that in order for me to move forward in life, I must muster up strength and confidence. I learnt not to allow challenges to defeat me.

At this stage of my life, even though I can say that I did find myself, and that I know who I am, it does not mean that this is the end of my personal growth.

I know I will continue to strive to be better, and continue to learn and grow. There is so much to learn in life that I know I can never stop learning. I have such a great thirst for knowledge that I am in constant awe of how situations arise for me, which lead me to learn and adopt new skills and knowledge.

This life and this world is filled with boundless information that is at my disposal. I feel it would be a shame to not take advantage of what is available to me.

I always like to encourage people to always be open to learning and growing on a daily basis. Learn to be a better person. Be the person you truly want to be—that is being your true self. When we can be our true selves, then we can just be who we are and not worry about keeping up with pretenses, or always trying to be someone we are not in order to adapt to what society wants us to be, and end up resenting ourselves.

Why Be Your True Self?

You may be wondering why I stress so much about being my true self. I spent the initial portion of my life living a life that was expected of me, a life based on what my parents wanted of me, and then the same followed in my married life. I was fairly young, and being an old soul, the life I was living didn't feel right, and it was not for me.

Living a life based on the expectations of others made me feel out of place. I felt like I was not allowed to be who I am, and I felt like I had so much potential buried deep within me. I had so much to offer, and yet it was buried and not allowed to come to the surface.

I was not really aware of all of this, but the initial feeling was that it didn't feel right. It didn't feel comfortable, which in turn made me feel unhappy and miserable.

Having faced so many challenges that life threw at me, I just knew that I needed to be me—I needed to be who I am in order to survive and overcome anything and everything that I would encounter.

I think it was then that I felt I needed to search within my soul; I needed to find out who it was that was buried deep within me.

It was life's challenges that led me to self-discovery, and they led me to find my purpose in life and what role I was to play in this lifetime. I learnt to find my purpose and my passion for what I really wanted to do with my life. Once I became aware of this, I began my journey.

My Journey to Being Me

How Did My Journey Start?

I can clearly say that when I started my journey, I really did not know that I had begun a new journey in being who I am. To me, at the time, it was simply a life I lived, adapting to the changes I needed to adapt to. In hindsight, I am able to say that my journey began then.

It began from the time I felt that I needed to adapt to the changes, to live the life I was living, making a change and growing according to what felt right and comfortable to me. Did my actions feel acceptable to me as a person, and could I feel happy and proud of my actions? Was I able to accept the consequences of my actions?

Giving deep thought to this, and knowing that some of my decisions and actions may not be acceptable or approved by those who were in my life, it still felt right to me. It was then that I felt that I was indeed being my true self, and traveling in my own journey in life.

Life's journey is compulsory, whether we want to go on one or not. It starts from the day we are born. We are not aware of our journey in the stage of infancy. We gradually realize that we are on some sort of journey as we become more aware of our lives and who we are, and the desire to know who we are and what our life purpose is.

That is the time when we can say that we are now in the quest to understand what our journey in life is. Many of us start to soul search, and to try to find meaning and purpose in life. That's when many consider that they are now on their life's journey. Prior to that, we are what we can consider to be "in the dark."

Why Does My Journey Continue?

After having gone through all the processes of learning and self-discovery, you would probably think that I should be done. I may have thought on rare occasions that I had really accomplished a lot and learnt a lot about life and how to manage any difficulties that I would be faced with, and that I really would not have much to worry about anymore. It would be like the saying: "Been there, done that." However, I feel that in life, we never stop learning.

For me, my thirst for knowledge is so great that I am always in awe of feeling that no matter how much I learn daily, it will never be enough. I thrive on constant learning. I feel that the more I learn, the more there is yet to learn.

Every single day of our lives is filled with new encounters and new experiences that determine our actions, which will ultimately affect us in ways that can either make our life's journey easy or difficult. Stay curious.

No matter what experiences we have, or where we work or what we would like to do over, life is a school, with so much potential to learn. The topics and subjects are endless. There is so much to learn that I will never stop learning till the day I die.

As soon as I have learnt something new, I am on another quest and am ready to learn something new. I am always seeking to learn something new. I know for a fact that if I did not, life would become meaningless. That is me, and that is who I am. I am that person that strives to improve themselves everyday—living the life of a seeker, and seeking knowledge.

New Realization

My journey continues even though I feel that I have found myself. Although I have learnt so much in life, I just never know what I can still learn about myself.

I have lived a fair number of years being in a very good place, where I can say that I have been a strong, independent woman, someone who has no trouble speaking her mind and standing up for herself, and being pretty fearless if I may say so; yet somehow, very recently, a new realization crept up, to my own surprise, that I still had some fear that I did not realize I had. It was the fear of being vulnerable to falling in love or being in love.

I know for a fact that I am a loving and kind person, but romantic love was something I really could not relate to, as I have never experienced it in the way most people described. I did not experience butterflies in my stomach, nor did I experience a strong desire for anyone; hence, I didn't understand when people talked about having strong chemistry. I may have experienced something but not strong enough to defy all logic.

I dated after my divorce, but somehow my mind and logic always made decisions as to how I wanted to proceed when meeting a potential partner. I have always been an analytical person, so I always analyze my relationships to avoid future problems. I analyzed my own personality compared to the person I was dating. If my analysis concluded that there was a potential conflict due to differences in how we viewed life, or how we would approach situations and challenges that we might encounter, then I felt it would be best to just be friends, and best not to explore a romantic relationship.

I think all this was possible because the connection was not undeniably strong. However, I did maintain a good friendship that I value very much.

I often hear of people describing the feeling of love at first sight, or how hopelessly people fall in love. So many stories have been historically written about love, and how love can lead someone to insanity.

I have encountered people in my life who were so broken-hearted when their relationship dissolved, and how helpless and hopeless they felt. I sympathized with the emotion but was unable to relate. I had no clue whatsoever, even though I felt their pain.

I often wondered why a person could not think and see for themselves that there were plenty of reasons and red flags, and yet could not avoid such red flags that were presented in front of them so that they could avoid falling into the pit of despair, or even setting themselves up for such grief.

I can now understand the terminology of the saying that has been around forever: "The heart wants what it wants or who it wants." Sadly, in cases like this, a person seems to not have much control over what they feel. The emotions seem to take over a person's logic, and the logic is thrown out the window.

The person in love is now at the mercy of the emotion and of a strong connection that is unexplainable, and we can even term it as a chemical connection, which people describe as having chemistry between them. That is why there are so many stories of relationships with people that are so not compatible, personality-wise.

People in love are so blind to all the red flags that are present, and they blindly get into relationships. When the connection is felt from one end, it is so easy for the other person on the other end to take advantage of what that other person feels. Hence, that is why it is so common for people to fall prey to undesirable circumstances.

When a person is lonely and feels such a connection, they can easily be a victim of being scammed.

Hidden Fear

This newfound fear that I never realized I had, was something that I felt I now needed to face, because all along I had always thought I was past any fears, and I was proud of the fact that I was pretty fearless. I must say that I was even proud of the fact that there wasn't really anything I feared.

When I first experienced instant connection with someone, it really took me by surprise, and I struggled to process this new experience that I was feeling. I even tried to analyze and understand it, but sadly, I really had nothing of substance to go by, or even had enough time with the person to even analyze and process this strange new feeling that I was feeling.

As time progressed, and having some contact even though it was purely a business relationship, I began to experience butterflies in my stomach. I had often wondered what it really felt like as described by many people who felt some kind of soul connection. I felt I could not understand or remotely relate to what people were describing.

For years, or I would say most of my life, I often felt that there was something wrong with me, because I was incapable of really relating to people that were going through a breakup with their romantic partner. I began to feel that I may be cold and heartless, even though I knew full well that I was not. Yet when I examined myself and my life, I knew that I was a loving and caring person, and that I am in fact capable of deep love and compassion; but in areas of romance, I simply could not relate.

Since I already knew that I was not like most people, and having the gifts that I had, I thought that perhaps that was the reason why I didn't feel what the entire population felt and experienced. I thought I was immune to such emotion or experience. I did feel love and some type of connection, but not one where I could say that it was unexplainable.

I felt that the reason may be because I wasn't born to experience that, and because I was meant to spend my life in solitude. I had spent nearly two decades of my life being content with my life of solitude. I simply had no desire to meet a life partner. I often felt the need to have my time of solitude so that I could recharge and be able to help those in need.

When I first felt this connection and felt the bond growing, I felt that I had been so used to living a life of solitude that my life of complete independence would be disrupted. Suddenly, I felt that I had lost control of my life, my thoughts, and my emotions, and I could not talk myself out of feeling what I felt. I started to fear that I did not have the ability to stop feeling what I felt. That was when I feared that I would experience the intensity of a broken heart like what was described to me by many for many years, which I was not able to really relate to.

I now began to understand what people felt when they were broken-hearted. I started to understand what people meant when they would say how broken-hearted they were. Even though I was not in a relationship, I could understand the emotion, which I never understood before.

I did not have any relationship with the person I felt connected to. I understood what it felt like to be broken-hearted. Even though I was not in a relationship, I somehow felt the discomfort in my heart. I now understand why people tend to feel bitterness and guardedness when that happens. I now understand why there is a saying that people lose their sanity. The emotions are too strong for the logic to play a part.

The friendship we developed was basically just conversational and nothing more, and yet it felt deep, and it was unavoidable how it was affecting me emotionally. No amount of intellect that I possessed could prepare me or help me avoid what I was experiencing emotionally. It felt like it was beyond me, and there was nothing I could do to prevent myself from developing feelings that were new to me.

Dealing With New Fear

With all this emotion swelling inside of me, it made it even more difficult to talk myself out of what I felt, so that I could protect my heart from being broken.

I am now faced with this new fear of having my heart broken, and I honestly have no idea if I can actually prevent myself from experiencing it. It was odd that it was even possible to think about having my heart broken, when there was no relationship of any sort. The friendship that grew was merely a conversation, and that was over the telephone. There was not even much interaction in person, yet the connection felt strong.

This is one fear that I feel is not an easy one to overcome, because it defies all logic. I also feel that it may be the most difficult one to deal with because it deals with an emotion that I feel is so consuming. It is no wonder that so many heartbreaking stories have been written about it.

I have been trying to understand, but no amount of intellectual or analytical capabilities I have are being helpful. The feelings are so intense that I even feel a lump in my throat, which I am unable to get rid of.

I have heard so much about all these emotions, and they were being described to me in countless measures. I hear so much about how people fear allowing others into their lives, for fear of being hurt or heartbroken. People build walls to prevent themselves from getting hurt. I know that I myself built a wall to prevent myself from being hurt or taken advantage of, but at the time, I did not even imagine being hurt in this manner.

I built walls to maintain my independence. I did not want to be a burden to anyone, as I was struggling with many health issues. I never wanted to be indebted to anyone. I wanted to be able to run my life as I pleased. All of this was possible and easy because it was not easy for me to be attracted initially to anyone solely on a physical level. For me, intellect played a stronger role than a physical one did.

Being a person who lived in my head most of my life, and who led my life using logic and intellect, life took a turn, and I started to learn to trust my instincts, so I combined these two traits of mine and lived my life accordingly.

Life began to have a new twist. I learnt to follow my inner guidance, and the more I learnt to trust my inner guidance or instinct, things started to flow smoother for me. I felt more at peace, and I felt more content.

Even though I feel I am now faced with a new fear of a new form of emotion swelling inside of me, and even though I feel the discomfort in my heart of what I feel—a feeling that no logic can explain; and a feeling that no matter how much I do not want it to reside in me, I am willing to accept it—I can now say that I finally do experience what the rest of the world experiences and feels.

I now no longer am a person who is incapable of relating to what others are feeling when they go through a broken heart. For now, I think having this new experience helps me to be in a better position to understand others even more.

Having this new experience helps me to have even more compassion towards those who are going through a broken heart, than I had before this newfound emotion. I am no longer wondering what it is like to be in their shoes, and the compassion that I feel for them is now going to be far deeper than before.

This experience has opened my eyes to what I feel is a new world to me.

To have the knowledge is one thing, but to actually have the feeling of it is completely another story. I feel that this now makes me a person who is whole and alive, a person that feels it all.

Overcoming This Fear

With the realization of this newfound emotion and fear, it was now up to me to find a way to overcome this fear. I am currently experiencing this newfound emotion. How do I feel about this? Am I capable of overcoming this fear—the fear of being vulnerable, the fear of being destroyed by this new emotion?

After doing some soul searching, I have concluded that I do not know what the future holds for me in this regard, but I do know that I do not intend to allow anything to hold me back from being my true self. I know that I want to have full charge of my life.

I feel that as difficult and uncomfortable this newfound emotion may feel, I intend to take charge of how I want to move forward with my life. I may not be immune to feeling the pain of not having my feelings reciprocated, but I am and should be in control of how I should and must react to such circumstances.

I have always been in a position where people come to me for moral support for all types of circumstances they go through, and therefore it is important for me to continue to be so. This situation has given me a new challenge to overcome.

As uncomfortable as this emotion may feel—a tightness in my chest and a lump in my throat, and a desire to delve into this feeling, deeper and deeper—I also know that this will not serve me for any purpose, and it will not be beneficial for me. The only thing it will do is handicap me from living a life of purpose.

I just know I cannot allow myself to be consumed by something that will destroy me and the purpose I am on this earth for. I must not be a hypocrite. I must practice what I preach. I must overcome my fears— all and every kind of fear that life throws at me.

I know for sure that no matter how much I may have learnt about myself up until now, I will continue to learn more and more about myself and my life's progress.

I know for a fact that I now feel that I have managed to learn how to be in charge of my life, and I have learnt many ways to overcome fear and to gain strength from life's challenges that I have been presented with. Having all these experiences does however help me to overcome new challenges more easily than in the past.

Having the knowledge that I have overcome all obstacles that life presented, I have the comfort of knowing that I am ready to take on any new challenge that I may encounter in the future. I would like to share with you that no matter what curve ball life may throw at you, do not be afraid to tackle it, for there is always a solution. If there is no solution, there is a way to handle it.

I made sure that I did not let any circumstances defeat me, no matter how difficult or painful they may have been. I carried on till I overcame them. It was not easy, but I had faith to carry on, and through determination and sheer focus, I pushed through the raging storms till the storms settled.

Having the determination to weather the storms, I had the opportunity to see the rainbows when the sun surfaced. The sun is bound to come up, if we allow ourselves the opportunity to let the storms pass. For every negative, there is always a positive.

We must always be in charge of our lives, and be authentic and be our true selves.

Chapter 10

How I See Life

Compiling of views of life in different ways:

The meaning of life has always been a big topic for me. Having had the life I had, I have always felt a need to express my pain and experiences to find comfort for my soul.

My habit of expressing myself was always through analogies, and I found it so much easier to do so this way. Expressing myself metaphorically is also another method that makes it so much easier to make sense of what is within me that needs to be formulated outward.

Over the years, I have written material about life, which includes poetry, and I would like to share this here to conclude my book.

Life Is Like a Painting

How do our lives have an effect on others? Our lives are all intertwined.

When we are born into this world, our lives are like a blank slate or a blank canvas.

Once we enter into this life, we start to paint a picture, little by little, and details are put onto the canvas. Sometimes while painting (as we go on with our lives), we may accidently lose the balance of our hands, and we may ruin a bit of the picture—we lost our strokes, and the fine details were lost or smudged. In order to correct the accidental mistakes, we sometimes have to have patience and wait for the paint to dry so that we can paint over it. The colors, when applied over other colors, create a distinct new color. Therefore, in life, when we go through experiences, it's like the colors of a pallet: When we make mistakes and repaint with new details, it gives us a new distinctive outlook in life, in comparison to when we don't make an error in our paintings.

We can either be so inspired to paint over our mistakes and create a beautiful masterpiece, or we can simply get irritated and think that the mess in the painting cannot be repainted into a new masterpiece (which is like having no hope). We then either choose to throw out the painting (giving up), or we simply keep painting over it without giving proper care and attention, because one thinks that no matter what one does, the ugliness of the painting is going to show through, and it will.

However, when one views the smudged part of the painting carefully, the artist will be able to see how, by careful choice of colors, he can create a new, beautiful masterpiece. Making careful choices in life makes us who we are.

Life is a painting. People are the colors, and the smudges and accidents are the mistakes we make and the experiences we have in our lives. When certain colors are combined together, they create a certain distinct color. This means that people in our lives, of different personalities and characters, can influence our personality, just as society or the social setting surrounding us influences who we are.

Just like a color, no matter how we mix them, we are still able to know the base color. No matter how much others may influence us, we are still who we really are. If you don't mix too many other colors, then the base color is generally prevalent.

When we don't allow others to influence our basic principles of who we are, then we are always able to shine our true colors.

Life is just as complex as a painting, with so many details and so many variations of colors.

If we choose to paint a beautiful picture, we will have a beautiful picture. When we paint with passion and interest in creating a beautiful picture or painting, that's what we will have. Therefore, we choose how we want our life to be, by being conscious of how we live it, and of the choices we make, despite experiences and setbacks.

When we are painting a masterpiece that we have a vision of, we must be sure to do the work ourselves; we cannot allow anyone else to get involved in the painting, unless it is someone who has the same vision as ourselves of how we want to create the masterpiece. If someone who does not have the same vision gets involved, or if we allow them to have their hand in the painting, the outcome will not be what we originally had hoped or planned for.

Therefore, we must decide how to handle our own lives. If we allow negative people to affect us negatively and to influence our happiness, then we are responsible for our own happiness. Hence, the painting may not be beautiful. However, if we don't allow others to affect us negatively, and we carry on with our own positive mindset, then we will be able to create our own future as we plan or want—a positive one.

We can allow others to give us advice and suggestions as to how to use colors or ideas, and then we can use our own vision to see if those suggestions will help us create what we want. If we allow ourselves to be open to suggestions and advice as to how we can handle and cope with our situations, some may be helpful and some may not. We are the only ones that will know what will help us grow and improve to be a better person, and what will not.

Although sometimes we may not be quite so aware of how to paint a beautiful picture, that's why we need good teachers to teach us. A good teacher will always be one that will try to teach and bring out the best in their students, and to teach them to create their own unique masterpiece.

Hence, having the right teacher is important and crucial to paint a beautiful picture or a painting.

Experience Life to the Fullest

When someone says, "Experience life to the fullest," what do they usually mean to say? Or how would one generally interpret it? In my observation of the general public or people I have encountered, I have come to the assumption that the phrase, "Experience life to the fullest," or, "Live life to the fullest," would generally mean for a person to experience life in the way that person would like to, or to do what they love to do, which could be a hobby or what they want in a career, or what they always dreamed of doing in life—the list can be endless, as everyone here on earth has different desires, skills, and talents.

To give an example, some people may have a passion for music, but different people with the same passion will do different things with that passion. Therefore, to each of them, experiencing music in life will be different. For some, they will pursue music as their career; whereas for others, they would like to be able to attend as many concerts as possible because of their love of music, but they do not have or possess the skill to play music.

Everyone has multiple interests and passions in life, so they would strive to achieve as many of these interests as possible in order for them to consider having experienced life to the fullest. Fulfilling one's bucket list may be what one may consider as experiencing life to the fullest.

What does *experiencing life to the fullest* really mean?

When we first enter this world, we never know what to expect, as we do not know what or who we will encounter in our lives. From the time we are born, we start experiencing life, but we are not even aware that we are experiencing life.

We are born with different senses through which we experience life. Predominantly, we are born with 5 senses: smell, sight, hearing, taste, and touch. Therefore, we experience all these five senses, and they are a part of living or being alive—hence, a part of life.

Every day, people are experiencing life, yet they are not fully aware of their experiences, as many take life for granted, going through life unaware of what life really is. Many go through it, not knowing what life is all about, and they carry on with their lives, fulfilling the expectations of others, or just fulfilling day-to-day expectations.

Some people go through life without many challenges, and they have a tendency to take life for granted until they are faced with a life threatening experience, or given news that they have an illness and that their life is now suddenly shortened. Such incidences tend to awaken many people, and they start to view life differently. Those who have taken life for granted, generally will start to appreciate life more after having a close call.

Then there are also others who have always been dealt challenges in life, and they resent the life they have; they cannot handle the challenges because of how the experiences of these challenges feel— they are too hard to handle. They then have the tendency to either end their life because they do not want to experience what their life has dealt them, or they choose to get into self-destructive behavior and get into addictions to numb the feelings of their experiences. They end up losing themselves, and they lose the desire to experience life. There are of course various reasons for this course of action that people take. For some, they may not possess an inner strength; and for some, they need support to help them deal with such challenges; and yet for some others, there may be some neurological deficiency to help them cope with life issues.

Sadly, for some people who are in such a situation and are not aware of their need for help for support in dealing with life, they are not so lucky to experience life to the fullest. Hence, they may either end up becoming an addict, trying to numb themselves, or committing suicide. Sometimes some of the people, if they get lucky and get the support they need to deal with life issues and challenges, may still have the possibility to experience life a bit more than they would have. Some could even have their life turned around, and they could learn to appreciate life and then set out to try to experience life fully.

There are also those who may have the very same challenges but accept all the experiences the challenges provide, who are also born with some inner strength, so they learn to be strong and to appreciate every experience that life offers. These are people who I believe actually experience life to the fullest, because they appreciate every experience of life. Life is filled with challenges and wonderful experiences. These are the people who understand that because they can experience some sadness, they know how to appreciate happiness. They can appreciate comfort because they know what challenges feel like. So, this is to say that one can experience life to the fullest when one is aware of all the good and bad experiences that life offers, and they can make the most of it. They accept the challenges gracefully and face them, and they still appreciate the experiences that the challenges teach them. They are grateful for the good things that life offers them. These are the people who truly are willing to experience life to the fullest.

Life and Love

Life is a four-letter word, yet when we are to describe what it means to us, there is an endless way to do so. What is life? What do we want to do with our lives? What do we want to achieve in life?

L. Living
I. In
F. Focus
E. Everyday

L. Longing
I. Incessantly
F. For
E. Everything

L. Listening
I. Intensely
F. For
E. Exquisite Music

We can go on and on about what it means to us individually, according to where we are at spiritually.

We always hear the saying that life is too short, and therefore we must make the most of what we have. When we say that life is short, we are referring to this physical life that we are living. But spiritually, souls live on. The life of a soul is not a short one, but I think we should still make the most of it.

When I say "make the most of it," I mean that we must try to do the best we can to do good in all our physical lives, in order to grow spiritually.

Then there is also the discussion about *karma*. It has been said that how we live our physical life somehow affects our next physical life. It is said that if we don't do good deeds in one physical lifetime, then we may pay the consequences in the next lifetime.

However, I think that if we do our best and be loving and kind to our fellow man, be of service and help those that need us, be ready to forgive those that hurt us, and continue to love those in need of love, then chances are that we won't even have to worry about karma.

Some may say that we are just humans, and that it's not possible for us to be good and loving all the time. There may be some truth to it because as humans, we do have all kinds of emotions, and therefore we may experience love, anger, hatred, disappointments, etc. However, I feel that if we fill our hearts with love, it leaves very little room for negative emotions; and even if we may experience this, it cannot stay long in our hearts, as there simply is no room for it because it's already filled with love, and it's the overflow that rids it of any negativity that may try to enter, as it leaves with the overflow.

Love

Love is also a four-letter word, just like life, and different people have different perceptions of love.

Different people feel love differently. Some may feel love for others but only if their needs are met by others, be it material or physical. Then there is that spiritual love, where we are love, and we love all those around us unconditionally. We love them because they are also a spiritual being in a physical body, just like ourselves.

We may not like them for their actions, yet we still love them for who they are, with all their faults. They may be unkind to us and hurt us, yet we are ready to forgive them and be there for them when they need us. Because we are filled with so much love and want to be of service to others, it does not matter what they may have done to hurt us, as love in our hearts erases the hurts and injustice inflicted upon us.

Love is a powerful energy. It has been said that love heals all wounds. It usually refers to emotional wounds.

Reiki, Qigong, and all other energy healing modalities are considered to be the energy of love. These energy healing modalities are known for helping different ailments, from the physical to the emotional. Ailments, although they may be physical, are sometimes manifested due to our emotions, caused by the daily stress of life.

Hence, the energy of love is considered powerful; so much so that it helps relieve us of the many ailments that we may experience.

The power of love also acts like a magnet, as it draws in goodness in people, and brings people, family, and friends together. As we all know, hatred has a tendency to pull people apart.

If love is the basic principle of our lives, then there is harmony amongst us. Love is light; hence, where there is light, darkness cannot exist. The two cannot cohabit. Therefore, if we choose light, there is love; and thus, there is no hatred or darkness.

When we practice love, we raise our vibrations so high that we can ascend to a fifth dimensional plane, where love flows naturally, we feel lighter, and negativity does not bring us down as easily as it would when we are in three dimensional planes.

Life Is a Journey

Life is a journey; when we first start, we do not know what our destinations are, but we do know or are aware of what options are available to us. When we first embark on our journeys, we are first learning about the different destinations ahead of us, just as a child learning to walk or talk, etc.

When we first start, our journeys are easy. As a child may have no responsibilities, life for a child may be generally easier. As we get older and become more aware of our surroundings and responsibilities, this is when we are faced with different choices of destinations. For some, the path to their destination may not be a smooth one; for others, it is a breeze. Different people choose different modes of transportation and where they want to go.

How a person's journey is going to be will likely depend on the destination they choose. However, we must keep in mind that the weather conditions can also have an impact on our journey, no matter what mode of transportation we may choose to take.

Some people may feel at a loss as to what their destination is, so they go on a quest in search of their destination, which for many leads them to a spiritual path, and on a spiritual journey. When our soul advances, we tend to take the spiritual route, which is more on a higher plane. Meanwhile, there are those that still need to learn lessons on this earth plane, so their journey will be different.

Destiny

People seem to have this notion that our destiny is carved in stone from the time we enter into this world. It is of the assumption that God writes our destiny. Why do you think people like to say that God writes our destiny? People have a tendency to shove responsibilities in their lives on to someone else other than themselves; it's better to blame God who created us.

If things do not go the way they hope, they blame it on someone else, because it's easy to, and it also frees them from being responsible for their own actions.

In reality, we write our own destiny. God created us and gave us free will to choose the life we want. He gave us free will to choose between good and bad, so how is it God's fault when things go the way they do? The outcome of our lives is based on the choices and decisions we make.

When we make decisions and act upon them without giving much thought to the consequences of our actions, we must hold ourselves accountable for the outcomes in our lives. We are the ones who create our destiny. As human beings, we are not perfect; we can make mistakes, so we can learn from them. If we accept the responsibilities of our mistakes, there is a good chance that we can learn a lesson from them, and we can make improvements.

One belief that I have in life is to have no regrets. When making any decision, think carefully of all possible outcomes from the decisions made. If the result of the outcome is not something that we had hoped for, or is not right for us at the time, it is best not to regret it or blame yourself for making a bad decision. Blaming oneself will not help one's growth, but rather it could stunt one's own growth because they would be wallowing in self-pity and not move on.

Drive to Destination of Life

You are the driver in the vehicle of life, and you need full control of your steering wheel in order to drive to the destination you choose for your life. Taking on passengers is your choice. A journey with a passenger in your vehicle will have a variable outcome.

Sometimes a passenger may only travel a short distance, and it can be a pleasant journey. Sometimes it may not be all that pleasant, but fortunately, the journey was a short one.

Sometimes you may have started with the intention of going to the same destination, but you soon realize that your personality does not click, and your journey starts to become a bit uncomfortable or unpleasant. The passenger may prove to be immature or unstable; so much so that the passenger may interfere with the steering wheel, causing the ride to be bumpy or to even potentially lead to a serious life threatening accident.

It's up to you to choose to make a quick stop and let the passenger get out of the vehicle, to prevent heading to a potential disaster, or you can carry on your trip and tolerate such behavior, and face the consequences of a potential fatal disaster.

Moving forward in your journey as you resume your trip, it is best not to go over it in your head about the journey you just had with the passenger that you just dropped off, or to be consumed by the drama that was created. All these distractions that you carry in your head can also lead to a disaster, which will then set you back, and you will need time to recover and heal before you can carry on with your journey.

It is important to concentrate on the road ahead, as hard as it may be. Continue on, with a new focus on the road map with which you have planned ahead towards your destination.

When you pay attention to the road that will lead to the destination you wish to reach, you will get there for sure.

However, during your journey, the road may not always be smooth and well paved, but you know that it will lead to where you want to go. Then you just have to drive carefully and patiently according to the road conditions, to get to where you planned to reach.

Along the way, you have a choice to pick up another passenger if you wish. Bad experiences in the past do not guarantee that you will continue to have bad experiences. You may even find a passenger who may go a long distance with you if you allow yourself to take that chance, which could be a fun and meaningful journey.

Or you can choose to enjoy your trip solo, in a calm and peaceful atmosphere as you wish. Ultimately, how you choose to drive to your destination is entirely your choice.

Life is all about having choices and having the courage to take chances, and having faith and hope. You decide for yourself what you want for yourself in life. Do you want your destination to be peace and happiness? Then it is your choice to map your route. The roads that you will take are the roads named love, forgiveness, sharing, caring, faith, hope, courage, and determination.

You Know You Are Blind When ...

The world is big and wide,
Filled with trees, mountains, and ocean tide.
Nature is filled with beauty of every kind,
Yet you do not see; that's when you know you are blind.

The world is filled with people of all kinds.
You cannot tell the difference, for you do not use your mind.
That's when you know you are blind.

Every day in our lives, there are people we meet,
Be it at work, at gatherings, or on the street.
Some of these we love to greet.
Some may be rude, cruel, fake, or kind.
When you cannot tell the difference, you know you are blind.

Day to day, you have someone around you, who is there,
For you and to be with you when your heart needs a mend,
And yet you say you don't have a friend.
All the while, this person has been nothing but gentle and kind,
Yet you don't really truly acknowledge it in your mind.
That's when you should know you are blind.

Take Charge

You think you are smart and know it all.
It's the one mistake that will make you fall.
For there are many things still to learn and understand,
But your ego stops you from learning all that you can.
All you think is how smart you are in your mind,
That's what makes you totally blind.

You like the people from whom you think you can take, take, and take.
You don't realize that someday this will be your big mistake.
All the while you think you are great, but sadly all has been fake.
When you lose people in your life that have been real and kind,
That's when you know you have been blind.

Desperately you seek someone to fill your desires and needs.
You are presented with all the red flags of the person's bad deeds.
Yet your desperate need makes you think you don't mind,
That's when you know you are blind.

You have people around that care about you all the time.
You do not see and act as if you don't give a dime.
You think all is good; things with them will always be fine.
When things fall apart, it never crossed your mind,
That's when you know you've been blind.

If you have someone whom you hold close and dear,
They will always be there to help take away tears and fears.
Always remember to keep them in mind.
Make sure, in this case, you don't be blind.